MADAME GANDHI

MADAME GANDHI

A Political Biography

By

DR. MITHRAPURAM K. ALEXANDER

Advisor, United Nations Volunteer Educational Unit
Chairman, Humanities & Philosophy Department
Arkansas State A.M.&N. College

THE CHRISTOPHER PUBLISHING HOUSE

NORTH QUINCY, MASS. 02171

Dedicated to

The Prince of Peace

PREFACE

I wish to express my heartfelt gratitude to Dr. S. Radhakrishnan, former President of India, for his interest and helpfulness which enabled me to have better insight into India's national and international problems.

I have spent almost two years in writing this biography. During this time, I have been able to bring together the experiences of my many years in India, in education and politics, and my years in the United States as an educator and spokesman for India's freedom struggle. During the year 1966, and in the summer of 1967, I toured India and visited with people from all walks of life, from the President on down to the village dweller. In addition, I have drawn information from my personal contacts with Mahatma Gandhi, Jawaharlal Nehru and other leaders in India's freedom struggle.

I am particularly grateful to the celebrated subject of this biography for her cooperation in making the work possible.

Many organizations and individuals both in and outside the government have generously assisted me in gathering materials for this work. Among them special mention must be made of the Ministry of Information and Broadcasting, the Indian Embassy in Washington and several friends and associates of Mrs. Gandhi. I am deeply indebted to Mr. H. Y. Sharada Prasad, Deputy Information Advisor to the Prime Minister, for the supply of literature of great value to my research. A special word of thanks is due to Mrs. Maurice T. Moore, Dr. B. A. Garside, Dr. V. M. John, Dr. H. T. Muzumdar, Mr. Victor Shukla and Mrs. Anne Schneider for their helpfulness in this effort. The author wishes to thank the following educators for reading the manuscript and offering valuable suggestions: Dr. R. C. Perry, Dr. D. D. Demecs, Mr. Will Bert Evans, Mr. Peter Johnson, Mr. and Mrs. Bert Carleton and Miss Rozanne Eubanks. (I am profoundly appreciative of the most valuable research assistance given by Dr. D. D. Demecs.)

I wish to thank the following persons for stenographic assistance: Mrs. Sarojini McGhee, Mrs. Annie Carter, Miss Thressa Hearring, Miss Franciene J. Gill and Mrs. Betty Carleton.

Words are inadequate to express my appreciation to my mother, Mrs. Aleyamma Kuryan, my wife, Mrs. Aley Alexander, and my daughter, Annimol, for their fervent support in my endeavours.

Above all my heart rises in salutation to the source of wisdom and knowledge, the "wonderful counselor, the mighty God, the everlasting Father, The Prince of Peace."

MITHRAPURAM K. ALEXANDER

FOREWORD

Indira Gandhi's father, Jawaharlal, and her grandfather, Motilal, were both active in India's independence struggle in the first three decades of the twentieth century. Their names are, therefore, mentioned often in the first two chapters of the book and they are usually referred to as Jawaharlal Nehru and Motilal Nehru. Later, however, after Motilal's death in 1931, Jawaharlal is generally mentioned by his last name only. Thus, during the greater part of the 1930's, the 1940's and the 1950's, the designation Nehru understandably refers to Jawaharlal Nehru and not to his father.

CONTENTS

CHAPTER I

FAMILY TREE

"The girl," exclaimed the man, rushing out of the Parliament House in New Delhi. In his hurried exclamation he was answering the questions of the swelling crowd, which was loudly asking, "Is it the boy or the girl?"

"Hurrah! It's the girl," rose the chants.

The day was January 19, 1966, a big day of election and expectation. The Parliamentary Party of the Indian National Congress had gathered to elect a new leader in the place of the late Prime Minister Lal Bahadur Shastri. The huge crowd of men, women and children gathered in the square outside the Parliament House eagerly awaited the outcome. The results, however, were as expected. Indira Gandhi polled 355 votes. Her opponent, Morarji Desai, a former Finance Minister, received 169.

Inside the Parliament House, Indira moved briskly towards the rostrum amidst the rousing applause of the parliamentarians. Before speaking she stood before them for a moment, and everyone sensed the aura of her natural, striking glow of beauty. On her brown sari she wore a red rosebud, reminiscent of her illustrious father, Nehru, who had led India through seventeen fateful years. Behind her warm

15

and gentle smile, they somehow could discern the indomitable spirit and courage that had marked her many years of service for her country. Then, in the elegant and transparent honesty for which she is noted, she spoke briefly in Hindi. "As I stand before you, my thoughts go back to the great leaders: Mahatma Gandhi, at whose feet I grew up, Panditji, my father, and Lal Bahadur Shastri. These leaders have shown the way, and I want to go along the same path."

Those who knew her closely recognized her humility; but at the same time, they knew that the new Prime Minister had a mind of her own. She would learn all she could from her associates; she would patiently listen to all sides of a dispute; but she would arrive at her own decision. They remembered what her father had remarked about his only daughter: "What am I to speak of Indira?" retorted Jawaharlal Nehru at a press conference on the occasion of Indira's election to the Presidency of the Indian National Congress. He had pointed out that her election was an indication that the congress was wide open to accept the services of youth and women and everyone who desired to serve the country. He had added that he was proud of her temperament, energy, affection and integrity—qualities which she had inherited from her mother. Later, in a Congress Party meeting held under her Presidentship, Nehru had remarked humorously that at first Indira had been his friend and advisor, next she had become his companion and then she was his leader.

The family tree of Indira Gandhi is traced to the Kashmiri Brahmins. According to tradition there was a famous man of learning in Kashmir called Pundit Raj Kaul. He was known as Pundit or Scholar because of his versatility in Persian and Sanskrit languages. It is said that the Mogul Emperor Farukhsiar visited Kashmir in the summer of 1716 for relief from the blistering heat of Delhi. While in Kashmir, he came to know of Pundit Raj Kaul. Because of his great regard for men of learning, the emperor sent for the Pundit on his return to Delhi.

When Raj Kaul came to Delhi with his family he was warmly welcomed and recognized as a scholar. He was given a house located on grounds near a canal. It is said that in order to identify the newcomers, the neighbors called them Kaul Nahar (the Kaul family on the canal). In time, the neighbors dropped the name Kaul and called them Nahar, which, in the course of years, was transformed into Nehru. This is how the Nehrus (the most widely known family name of India) evolved.

At Delhi, Raj Kaul and his offsprings prospered. One of the descendants, Pundit Lakshmi Nehru, served as a lawyer for the East India Company, a British firm that carried on trade in India. (This company eventually became politically powerful and laid the foundation for the British rule in India.) His son, Pundit Ganga Dhar Nehru, was appointed Police Commissioner of Delhi.

During the mutiny of the soldiers against the British, the family sold everything and fled to Agra. After they settled in Agra, in 1861, Ganga Dhar

Nehru died. A son, Motilal Nehru (father of Jawaharlal Nehru) was born seven months later. An
older son in the Nehru family was appointed to the
High Court in Allahabad and because of this appointment the family moved to Allahabad.

Motilal Nehru studied law and started to practice
in the Allahabad High Court. He amassed great
wealth and lived luxuriously. Jawaharlal, his only
son, was born to his very lovely wife, Swaruprani.
Motilal gave the boy the best education possible at
that time. Jawaharlal went to high school at Harrow
in England; he received his college education at Cam-
bridge and later became a barrister. He also acquired that special kind of education and experience
that comes from traveling widely in Europe.

Motilal Nehru once wrote to his son explaining
why he had done so much for his education. "It is
a question of making a real man of you, which you
are bound to be," he wrote. "I think I can, without
vanity, say that I am the founder of the fortunes
of the Nehru family. I look upon you, my dear son,
as the man who will build upon the foundation I
have laid and have the satisfaction of seeing a noble
structure of renown rearing up its head to the skies."
Needless to say, Jawaharlal fulfilled these expectations in a greater manner than the father expected.

Soon after Jawaharlal's return from England, his
father arranged a marriage for him (as was the
custom in those days among most Indians). The
bride was Kamala Kaul, a tall, slim beauty from an
orthodox Kashmiri Brahmin family. Although she
lacked the cosmopolitan background and training
of Jawaharlal, she adjusted herself, in due course,

to the new Indo-European environment of the Nehru family. She was intensely devout and religious at heart.

Motilal Nehru had hoped that his son would, after all the education he had in England as a barrister, lead a prosperous life at the bar. But the situation of the country blighted all such hopes. The people were gradually awakening to demand their birthright of freedom. Pioneer leaders like Annie Beont stirred the people by a clear call for "Home rule." The British government was alarmed. They passed repressive measures, such as the Rowlatt Acts, to destroy the freedom movement. Acting in accordance with the Rowlatt Acts, soldiers under O'Dwyer shot and killed nearly five hundred people in an attempt to disperse a protest gathering. This massacre created great horror in the land and, in fact, strengthened the freedom struggle. Soon thereafter, Jawaharlal dedicated his life to free his people from the foreign yoke. The father in due course followed his son.

Indira, the first and only child of Jawaharlal and Kamala, was born on November 19, 1917, in the midst of India's freedom struggle. Even as a child she was immersed in politics. She recalls attending her first political gathering at the age of three—in the arms of her grandfather, Motilal Nehru. However, during Indira's early years, her parents were often in jail or busy with political works. Thus, the lonely little girl was left to assemble and exhort her dolls to court imprisonment for the national cause. She was constantly bewildered by the spectre of her family members being led to prison, and much annoyed by witnessing the police seizing most of the belongings of their house. Concerning this, Jawaharlal wrote in his biography: "It was the Congress policy not to pay fines, so the police came day after day and attached and carried away furniture. Indira, my four-year-old daughter, was greatly annoyed at this continuous process of despoliation and protested to the police and expressed strong displeasure. I am afraid those early impressions are likely to color her future views about the police force generally."

Indira did not have many occasions to play with other children. "My favorite occupation," she says, "was to stand on a high table with servants gathered around me and deliver thunderous political speeches." In the absence of the great pastime of playing with other children, she assembled her dolls and instructed them in protest demonstration. In imitation of what was going on in the world outside, she would have other dolls rush in and take the demonstrators to jail.

Anand Bhawan, the palacial home of the Nehru family, soon became the nerve center and headquarters of the political struggle. All the great leaders like Mahatma Gandhi, Malaviya, Azad and Sarojini Naidu frequented the house. As a child Indira came in contact with these luminaries. She was a welcome visitor to their meetings and would sit and listen seriously for hours. Then she would go out, call the servants together and, seated on a table, harangue them with snatches from the talks she had heard at the conference of the leaders.

She watched great changes take place in her home.

The luxurious palace was transformed into an austere home for the dedicated workers of the freedom
movement. Selfless service for the country was the
main goal.

Young and old were asked to work unselfishly.
They were trained to be well disciplined, to bear
every form of hardship for the liberation of their
"mother land." Daily Indira would hear national
songs, the marching of the volunteers and many
stirring appeals for sacrifice for the country.

As part of the freedom movement, the achievement of self-reliance by the use of homemade goods
was advocated. To dramatize the importance of
this, the boycott of British goods was organized. The
pioneers of this movement were so emotional that
they began to ignite bonfires of the foreign goods
they possessed. Indira saw all the many costly
silks, fabrics and other British goods heaped in great
piles on the terrace of her home and burned.

A very touching story is told of one of the many
personal sacrifices that Indira had to make. She
had a very beautiful dress from Paris presented
to her by a relative. As a child, she wanted very
much to have this. Her mother let Indira decide for
herself and, true to the attitude of her parents,
she declined the present with thanks. The relative
teased her by asking why she played with a foreign doll if she would not accept a dress made in
Paris. This made Indira reconsider her doll. It
had become a part of her life. She loved it dearly
and yet the words of her relative hurt her conscience.
For days she walked about in deep thought with the
doll by her side. Finally, in step with the rigorous

call of the boycott, she went up to the terrace and threw the doll in the fire.

The atmosphere of the house was extremely distracting for the little girl. Great crowds would come there from all over the country. They would break out in loud slogans like "Jawaharlal Ki Jai" ("Victory to Jawaharlal"). Indira would wake up at night and listen. Often, her sleep was interrupted by the entry of police into the house, either to arrest the dwellers or to carry away the valuables—art collections, furniture and jewelry. These they would sell at auctions to realize the fines imposed on freedom fighters. Naturally, she was indignant and upset by this procedure. She would read the story of Joan of Arc and imagine that one day she, too, would ride with sword in hand to expel the British rulers from the country.

Her courage she patterned after her father's. Jawaharlal was one of the bravest of men. He taught the child to be unafraid. It is said that when she was a small girl, Nehru took her to the Frontier Province. It was well-known that the people there were tough mountaineers. They were hostile to strangers. However, Nehru took Indira with him and told the Pathans in the village far beyond Peshawar that he was going to leave the child with them while he went out for his work. "She is our child and we will protect her," said the Pathans in unison. And so they did. In these and other ways the father tried to develop courage and independence in his little girl.

Indira's education was a matter of great concern to her parents. Because of the national sentiment against all things foreign, they were reluctant to send her to an English School. Hence, she was kept at home under the guidance of tutors.

Recognizing the inadequacy of her schooling, Nehru decided to write letters to his daughter to enable her to have a broad-based education. His first letter of the series was written in 1928 (when Indira was eleven years old), while he stayed in the summer heat of Allahabad and Indira was sent to Mussoorie, a cool hill station. In that letter he said: "When you and I are together, you often ask me questions about many things, and I try to answer them. Now that you are at Mussoorie, and I in Allahabad, we cannot have these talks. I am, therefore, going to write to you from time to time short accounts of the story of our earth and the many countries, great and small, into which it is divided." These letters gave the youngster much information of the geological history of the planet, prehistoric man and world history. They also gave her the necessary perspective and inspiration for the freedom struggle to which she dedicated her life. Nehru's famous book *Letters From a Father to His Daughter* was the collection of thirty letters he wrote to Indira. In these letters, the father not only tried to inform the daughter, but also to inspire her to be a worthy soldier for India's freedom. "If we are to be India's soldiers," he wrote, "we have India's honor in our keeping, and that honor is a sacred trust. Often, we may be in doubt as to what to do. It is no easy matter to decide what is right and what is not. One little test I will ask you to apply whenever you are in doubt. It may help you. Never do anything in secret or anything that you would wish to hide. For the desire to hide anything means that you are afraid and fear is a bad thing and unworthy of you. Be brave and all the rest follows. If you are brave, you will not fear and will not do anything of which you are ashamed. You know that in our great Freedom Movement, under Bapuji's leadership, there is no reason for secrecy or hiding. We have nothing to hide. We are not afraid of what we do and what we say. We work in the sun and in the light. Even so, in our private lives, let us make friends with the sun and work in the light and do nothing secretly or furtively. Privacy, of course, we may have and should have, but that is a very different thing from secrecy. And if you do so, my dear, you will grow up a child of the light, unafraid and serene and unruffled, whatever may happen.

"You are fortunate, I have said in being a witness to this great struggle for freedom that is going on in our country. You are also very fortunate in having a very brave and wonderful little woman for your mummie, and if you are ever in doubt or in trouble you cannot have a better friend.

"Good-bye, little one, and may you grow up into a brave soldier in India's service.

"With all my love and good wishes."

Chapter II

AILING MOTHER

Kamala Nehru, mother of Indira, was a woman of great inner strength. She exercised enormous influence on her daughter's early life and education. In fact, Indira has often said that her mother was a greater influence in her life than was her father. Her mother inculcated in her a love for literature and an appreciation for India's cultural heritage. She also helped Indira develop the quiet courage and determination so characteristic of her career. Unfortunately, Kamala's activities were hampered by ill health and the development of tuberculosis.

It was Kamala's failing health, however, that was indirectly responsible for the incident that brought Jawaharlal into direct contact with the masses. In May of 1920, with both his wife and his mother in failing health, Jawaharlal decided to take them for a holiday to Mussoorie. It was in Mussoorie that his father, a lawyer, was busy on an important case. At the hotel where the Nehrus stayed were members of the Afghan delegation who had come to India to negotiate a peace treaty with the British following King Amanullah's brief war of 1919. Jawaharlal, having had no interest in them, never met them. But the British authorities feared that he might and asked him for an understanding that he

would have no dealings with them. Jawaharlal
thought this preposterous and refused. Thereupon
the government issued an externment order re-
quiring him to leave the district within twenty-four
hours, which he did. Subsequently the order was
rescinded and Jawaharlal returned with his father
to Mussoorie. However, the first person that greeted
him at the hotel was his baby daughter, Indira, in
the arms of one of the members of the Afghan delegation! They had read of the episode in the papers,
and, interested by it, started sending Jawaharlal's
mother a basket of flowers and fruits every day.

The freedom struggle continued under the leadership of Gandhi. In 1921, individual Congress
workers offered non-cooperation. They were arrested throughout the country. British officialdom
was becoming nervous and excited in the face of
non-violent non-cooperation. In order to build up
their morale they arranged a visit by the Prince
of Wales (the present Duke of Windsor) to India.
The Prince evidently was a popular figure. However, Congress organized a boycott of this effort
of the British Government to exploit the Prince's
popularity. Motilal and Jawaharlal were arrested.
Both received sentences of six months' imprisonment and fines of five hundred rupees each.

Jawaharlal was in Lucknow Jail until January 3,
1923, except for six weeks early in 1922. Little Indira was permitted to see him only once every three
months and her health caused him much concern.
Evidently she was suffering from mental depression

and lack of emotional security due to separation from father and grandfather.

To envelop her with his affection even from that distance he wrote letters to her. These letters were similar to the following one. "To dear Indu, love from her Papu. You must get well quickly, learn to write letters and come and see me in jail. I am longing to see you." Her grandfather had sent a spinning wheel to keep her occupied. The father for his part encouraged his daughter to spin and send some of the yarn she had spun. He enquired as to whether she joined her mother in prayers everyday. Despite all this attention Indira's health did not show improvement. She was ailing deep in her heart. Therefore, since this superficial sort of attention had done little good, she was taken for examination and treatment to Calcutta.

In 1922, while in jail, Motilal Nehru had founded the Swaraj (self-rule) party within the Indian National Congress. He wanted to fight the British from inside the legislature as well as from the outside. Gandhi continued the non-cooperation movement by boycotting legislatures. They met in 1924 to discuss their points of view but were unable to arrive at any agreement. Motilal at that time did not concur with Gandhi in the use of non-violence for the achievement of freedom.

As luck would have it, Jawaharlal did not participate in the controversy. He spent his time with his family. It gave him and the family great happiness. Indira was especially joyful because she was able to see a lot of her father, who had been away so long. Her Papu again walked with her and talked with her. They played games and had lots of fun together.

In 1924, Kamala gave birth to a baby boy. But the joy in Indira and her parents was marred by the baby's death one week after his birth. Thus ended Indira's dreams of a brother to brighten her long stretches of loneliness. It looked as though adversities came in crowds, for soon thereafter her mother's health began deteriorating.

In the autumn of 1925, Kamala's illness took a turn for the worse. She lay in Lucknow Hospital for months. Jawaharlal was then the General Secretary of the Congress. He had to make arrangements for the annual session of the Congress in Cawnpore. With the work of the Congress and the need to attend to his ailing wife, Jawaharlal was distracted and worried. He had to rush back and forth in a triangular route between Allahabad, Cawnpore and Lucknow. On the advice of several doctors, swift arrangements were made to take Kamala to Switzerland for treatment. Early in March, Jawaharlal, Kamala and Indira left Bombay by steamer to Venice en route to Geneva. With them on the same boat went his sister Vijayalakshmi and her husband R. S. Pandit. The family, especially Indira, enjoyed the voyage immensely. She played deck games with her father and in the evenings they would relax on the deck chairs. The father entertained the daughter with stories about the origins of life and stories about the great hero kings of Indian history, Ashoka and Akbar, or about the Great Revolutionaries who sacrificed their lives for the country's freedom.

Once in Switzerland the bracing climate of the Alps and the care of expert doctors gradually helped Kamala gain strength. The family spent most of their time in Switzerland, especially in Geneva and in a mountain sanatorium at Montana. Jawaharlal's youngest sister Krishna joined them. Together the family had some happy days among the mountains and lakes. They took to mountain climbing and winter sports, especially ice-skating and skiing. The father led Indira in these games, although as a novice at skiing he often had to pay a painful price. He said later that although it was a new experience, he "succumbed to its fascination. It was a painful experience for a long time, but I persisted bravely, in spite of innumerable falls, and I came to enjoy it."

At times when Kamala felt better, father and daughter traveled to London, Paris, Berlin and other cities. The ten-year-old girl was deeply impressed by the beauty and grandeur of the places visited. In her young mind, however, she often wondered at the contrast between the prosperous people of these cities and the poverty-stricken people of her homeland. Sometimes she felt inwardly troubled. Her father allayed her anxiety by pointing out to her that one day a free India would provide a happier future for its people. Yet, just as she was impressed by the glittering sights of these big cities, she was depressed by the dingy dwellings of the slums. She could not understand why there should be pockets of dire poverty amidst the vast panorama of wealth.

While her parents stayed in Europe, Indira

studied briefly in three different schools, including
the International School in Geneva and the Ecole
Nouvelle, the New School, in Bex. Whenever there
was time, either during holidays or between schools,
she enjoyed visiting with her parents. Sometimes
she accompanied her father to meet very interesting personalities, such as Romain Roland, Albert
Einstein, Ernest Toller, Bernard Shaw and Charlie
Chaplin. These contacts made a great impression
on young Indira. She admired her father all the
more for having the friendship of so many eminent
artists, scientists and statesmen.

In September, 1927, Motilal joined the family.
Leaving Indira at school, the family visited the
Soviet Union where they were specially invited
for the occasion of the Tenth Anniversary Celebra-
tions of the October Revolution (1917). On returning from Moscow the party stopped in Berlin. After
a brief stay they proceeded to Marseilles via Paris
and from there by steamer to Madras, India. It
was December, 1927, time for the Annual Session
of the National Congress. Kamala's health had
improved considerably and her husband felt more
relaxed and eager to plunge into politics.

Back in Allahabad, Indira started enthusiastically
in a program of social service. At the tender age
of ten she surprised her parents by going on a
bicycle every Sunday to a leper colony in Naini six
miles away to help the lepers. She visited the Hig-
ginbothams, American missionaries in Allahabad,
and joined them in their services to the poor.

Jawaharlal's travels enhanced his hopes for a
better future for India. He was more determined

than ever before that his country should have sweeping changes, both political and social. He said, "Two things are dear to me, independence for this country of ours and equality between man and man."

In 1928, soon after the All-Parties Conference in Bombay, Jawaharlal took Kamala and Indira to the Mussoorie hill station and then returned to the plains to join his colleagues in the political struggle. The British Conservative Government headed by Stanley Baldwin had sent a seven-man British Commission, under the leadership of Sir John Simon, to investigate and recommend further constitutional advances. The Congress organized a boycott of the Commission as it was not satisfied by its all-British composition and conservative approach to India's freedom struggle. Wherever the Commission went they were met by black flags and crowds shouting "Simon go back." The Government in turn beat up demonstrators in every city that the Commission visited.

On the first day small groups of sixteen went separately to their meeting place. A gang of mounted policemen bore down upon them and beat them with truncheons. They were pursued and beaten as they sought safety on the sidewalks. Many had bleeding and split skulls. As one mounted policeman approached, Jawaharlal turned his head away to save it and received two brutal blows on his back; he felt stunned, his body quivering all over. Yet he stood his ground. The police withdrew and blocked the road.

The next day they started on their procession to the railroad station. The previous incident had

aroused the people in Lucknow. Many of them
headed toward the station. The main procession
of several thousand, marching four abreast, started
from the Congress office, while numerous small
processions came from various other parts of the
city. As they approached the station the police
stopped them. The police, the military and many
sympathetic onlookers were in the huge open space.
Suddenly, two or three long lines of mounted police
and cavalry rode on the people in the procession,
galloping over them and striking innocent and harm-
less stragglers. The processionists were beaten
mercilessly. In Lucknow, Jawaharlal, who was
leading the demonstrations, was badly beaten by
mounted police with truncheons. Under a hail of
blows he stood his ground, bleeding profusely and
in severe pain. More blows came. He did not move
until his younger colleagues carried him off to safety,
much to his annoyance. They feared that he might
be beaten to death. That day the mounted police
acted with furious brutality. They mangled bodies,
breaking arms, legs and heads. But they could not
break the spirit of the people.

In the following year, 1929, Jawaharlal was chosen
President of the Congress. The historic Congress
session in Lahore had an attendance of 300,000
persons. It was held in a great tent on the bank
of the river Ravi in the last week of December. On
the first day there was a grand procession to the
meeting grounds. Jawaharlal rode on a white
charger accompanied by uniformed volunteers and
followed by a herd of elephants and vast concourse
of people. It was here that the Congress adopted

his resolution on complete independence, and decided
that January 26, 1930 should be observed as complete independence day. Everyone was exhorted to
repeat the independence pledge drafted by Jawaharlal. It rings true like the American Declaration
of Independence.

"We believe that it is the inalienable right of the
Indian People, as of any other people, to have freedom and to enjoy the fruits of their toil and have
necessities of life, so that they may have full op-
portunities of growth. We believe also that if any
government deprives the people of these rights and
oppresses them, the people have a further right to
alter it or to abolish it. The British Government in
India has not only deprived the Indian people of
their freedom, but has based itself on the exploita-
tion of the masses, and has ruined India economically, politically, culturally and spiritually. We believe
therefore that India must sever the British con-
nection and attain Purna Swaraj."

It so happened that Indira became one of the
first pledgees. She was observing her father prepare the draft. When he finished it he asked her to
read it. Her face beamed as she read it clearly,
forcefully, sincerely. When she concluded, her father looked at her and said, "You read it well,
Indu. But, do you realize that, by reading it aloud,
you too are now pledged?" Yes, she realized it with
all the fiery idealism of youth. But young Indira
could hardly foresee the many trials through which
she would pass before she could reach the eventual
goal.

Overnight, Jawaharlal became the hero of the

masses, the idol of young India. He was honored wherever he went. Songs were composed about him. Legends mushroomed around his name. In the many addresses presented to him such epithets as Bharat Bhushan (Jewel of India) and Tyagamurti (Embodiment of Sacrifice) were generously used. Some of this praise went to the head of the young man. He confesses in his autobiography that his wife and sisters teased him continually, and that it helped to trim him down. At the breakfast table one of them would mutter: "O Jewel of India, please pass the butter." Indira, joining in the good-humored raillery, would add, "O embodiment of sacrifice, you are dripping jam on the table cloth." These family jokes helped the leader with his "head in the clouds" to keep his feet on the ground.

On March 12, 1930, Mahatma Gandhi started the Salt Satyagraha as part of the civil disobedience movement. As he proceeded day after day thousands joined him in his walk to the sea at Dandi. He and his followers walked a distance of 241 miles. By the time they reached the sea, the following had swollen to a huge procession that attracted world attention. Gandhi boiled some sea water and made salt. This was token protest against the salt tax.

On April 6, (the day that Gandhi protested the salt tax law at Dandi) Motilal renamed his old house *Swaraj Bhawan* (house of independence) and presented it to the Indian National Congress. Jawaharlal, as President of the Indian National Congress, accepted the gift of the house from his father. Henceforth, it would serve as the headquarters of the Congress Party. The new house was named *Anand Bhawan* (abode of happiness).

Civil disobedience in the form of breaking the salt law continued. The movement expanded in many directions. Foreign cloth shops and liquor shops were picketed. The revolution swelled. Kamala and other ladies of Anand Bhawan joined in this protest. Very soon Motilal, Jawaharlal and Gandhi were arrested. While her husband was in prison, Kamala carried on Congress work in Allahabad. She gained considerable reputation as a public speaker and organizer. Everyone was impressed by her organizing ability and devotion to duty. Jawaharlal, himself, was pleasantly surprised by the vigorous campaigning carried on by his frail partner in the interests of the freedom struggle. She was a guiding light to him in the enveloping darkness. "Kamala surprised me," he wrote from jail, "for her energy and enthusiasm overcame her physical ill-health, and for sometime at least, she kept well in spite of strenuous activities."

Twelve-year-old Indira did not want to be a silent spectator. Evidently she had inherited the organizational prowess of her mother and the daring of her father. Out she went (uniformed in khaki tunic and trousers) and organized the Monkey Brigade which grew to have a membership of more than six thousand. It is reported that when the first meeting was held and Indira started talking amidst an excited gathering, her voice could not be heard very far. So, she asked a friend to repeat her words. This process of repetition was made by others until her voice, with the aid of the human "public address

system," reached the entire crowd. Indira's so-
called monkey brigade rendered most valuable service to the Congress by performing many kinds of
errands, putting up signs and notices, doing office
work, cooking food, giving first aid, making flags and
carrying messages. In some ways, as children, they
were able to carry out minor intelligence activity
for the Congress which adults could not. They would
innocently loiter around police stations to get news
of possible arrests and police movements. Whatever news they picked up they passed on to the
Congress. They were often successful in slipping
through police lines unnoticed and carrying messages to leaders in jail and, in turn, from them back
to relatives and friends. They also helped set up
shops to popularize handspun cloth and Indian made
goods.

Indira's grandfather was always inquiring about
her doings. He was pleased and gratified by the
news of his twelve-year-old Indu organizing a monkey brigade in the service of the Congress. His
sense of humor still intact, he wrote from jail:
"What is the position in the monkey army? I suggest the wearing of a tail by every member of it,
the length of which should be in proportion to the
rank of the wearer."

While in jail, Jawaharlal's thoughts often turned
to his only daughter and her education. Confidently, and sometimes overconfidently, he thought that
he could have handled this matter if he were free.
However, because of his detention, he continued her
education through correspondence by means of letters. With an occasional release, he was in jail

till 1933. The second series of letters ended on August 9, 1933. These were later published as *Glimpses of World History.* They certainly provided glimpses not only into world history but also into the inner world of the writer. The extensive scope of these letters gave his young daughter a good perspective of India's freedom struggle in relation to global history.

The rigorous routines of prison life bore down on the health of Motilal. His asthmatic condition grew worse. Jawaharlal nursed him very ably and diligently. However, the father's condition worsened and he was released on September 11, 1930. He was immediately taken to Mussoorie by his wife, daughters and Indira. Kamala stayed at Anand Bhawan and carried on party activities with renewed vigor and determination.

After another month Jawarharlal was released. Along with Kamala, he joined his father at Mussoorie. There he found Motilal much improved in health. Jawaharlal was relieved. He relaxed by playing with his daughter and Vijayalakshmi's three small girls. The five of them would huddle together and then march around the house in a procession waving Congress flags and singing.

It was not long, however, before Jawaharlal went to the plains again and joined the political melee. He exhorted the people to continue non-cooperation by non-payment of taxes. Traveling by car he addressed many gatherings. By this time his family had returned to Allahabad from Mussoorie. Jawaharlal and Kamala went to the railway station to greet them. Afterwards he and Kamala addressed

a peasant meeting. At the close of the meeting he
was arrested and marched off to prison. He received a prison sentence of two-and-one-half years.

On the imprisonment of his son, in October, Motilal assumed the presidency of the Congress, as
was desired by Jawaharlal. Motilal then issued an
order to the Congress to observe Jawahar Day on
November 14 (birthday of Jawaharlal) as a protest
against "the savage sentence of two-and-one-half
years."

Processions and meetings were held all over the
country in observance of Jawahar Day. A mam-
moth procession in Allahabad was led by Indira,
her mother, grandmother and some other members
of the family. At the meeting that followed, her
mother read the speech of Jawaharlal for which he
was sentenced.

On January 1, 1931, Kamala and other women
volunteers of the Congress were arrested and sent
to Lucknow Prison. Typical of Kamala's courage
and resoluteness was the statement she gave on
the spur of the moment to a reporter who asked
for a message. "I am happy beyond measure and
proud to follow the footsteps of my husband. I hope
the people will keep the flag flying." Her husband
in prison was proud and pleased. But, in his autobiography, he stated "She would not have said just
that if she had thought over the matter, for she
considered herself a champion of women's rights
against the tyranny of man!"

On January 26, Kamala was discharged from
prison after a jail term of twenty-six days. As
Motilal's health was fast declining, Jawaharlal also

was released in order that he might be with his father. Motilal was being attended by three eminent doctors. He was also cared for with tender affection by his son and wife.

Motilal maintained his courage and sense of humor till the end. He joked with his wife that he was going ahead to wait in heaven to receive her. He also added that he did not want anyone to pray for him because he who made his own way in this world hopes to do so in the next also! Pointing to the swelling on his head, he said, "have I not qualified for a beauty competition?" To Gandhi he said, "Mahatmaji, you have perfect control over your sleep. I have perfect control over my digestion; it never fails me."

Motilal's friend and co-worker, Mahatma Gandhi, sat by his side. Turning to the architect of the freedom struggle, Motilal said, "I am going soon, Mahatmaji. I shall not be here to see Swaraj (Self-Government). But I know that you have won it and will soon have it." Gandhi leaned forward and stroked his friend's hand. "We will have it, Motilal," he said. "Together we have worked for it, and partly because of it you lie here today. It is a great price paid for a precious article."

The end came on February 6. The funeral was almost a national day of mourning. A mighty concourse of people turned out for the cremation on the bank of the river Ganges.

Jawaharlal described it with deep feeling in these words: "As evening fell on the river bank on that winter day, the great flames leaped up and consumed that body which had meant so much to us

who were close to him as well as to millions in
India. Gandhi said a few moving words to the
multitude, and then all of us crept silently home.
The stars were out and shining brightly when we
returned, lonely and desolate." Indira looked the
loneliest and most bereaved; she loved her Dadu
(grandfather) very much. She was, in turn, the
apple of his eye.

Due to many years of strain and stress and constant imprisonment, Jawaharlal's health began to
fail. His doctors urged him to take a rest and get
a change. He decided to take his family and spend
a month in Ceylon (since it was within easy reach
of India). It was the first holiday that father, wife
and daughter had had since his return from Europe
in 1925. It was also the last they ever had together.
Indira enjoyed this holiday immensely. Her father
gave her a running commentary of the many places
of historic significance and scenic beauty that they
visited.

There was not much rest, except for two weeks
which they spent at Nuwara Eliya. People there
were very friendly and brought Jawaharlal and his
family many gifts, such as flowers, homemade butter
and vegetables.

They visited many places on the island. Jawaharlal particularly liked a seated statue of Buddha
at Anuradhapura. He had a picture of the statue
with him when he was in Dehra Dun Jail a year
later. The calm strong features of the statue gave
him strength while in jail. He recalled that it was
not a case of religious appeal, "It is the person-

ality that has drawn me. So also the personality of Christ has attracted me greatly.''

While in Ceylon he saw many Buddhist monks. He was impressed by their seemingly calm life with their faces free from conflict. But he knew that his life was to be ''cast in storms and tempests.'' He also realized that he might not be content if he found himself ''in a safe harbor, protected from the fury of the winds.'' It was in his nature to take risk for causes he cherished. The greater the risk, the greater appeared the challenge for him.

Leaving Ceylon they went to South India, to the southern tip at Cape Comorin. It was very peaceful there. They traveled through Travancore, Cochin, Mysore, Malabar and Hyderabad (these were Indian States). Travancore with its evergreen landscape, many rivers, lakes, seacoast and extensive coconut groves has been called the garden of India.

While in Cochin they saw one of the ''White Jew'' services in their old tabernacle. The community was unique and ancient. The inhabitants were refugees from Palestine who fled during the invasion of Israel by the Babylonians. They received a warm welcome and found life in Cochin prosperous and peaceful. Their part of the state resembled ancient Jerusalem.

There were some towns along the backwaters of Malabar that were inhabited mainly by Christians of the Syrian churches (the Marthoma, Jacobite and Catholic denominations). Christianity had come to India during the first century. It established a firm hold in South India. It is believed that Thomas the apostle of Christ was the messenger of the gospel (of love of God and love of one's neighbor as one-self) to South India in about 54 A.D. During the long course of its history, the Marthoma Church founded by St. Thomas came under the influence of the Nestorian Church, the Roman Catholic Church and the Jacobite Syrian Church. Today a reformed section of the community maintains its identity as the Marthoma Church.

Jawaharlal came across a Nestorian colony in the south. Their bishop told him that there were about ten thousand members in his diocese. This surprised Jawaharlal because he was under the impression that other sects had long before absorbed the Nestorians.

The vacation lasted for seven weeks. Returning home in May, 1931, Jawaharlal again plunged into the whirlpool of Congress politics. In June, Indira was admitted to the Pupils' Own School in Poona.

CHAPTER III

SCHOOLING AND EDUCATION

Indira's schooling and education had two outstanding characteristics. One was the influence of
prominent personalities inside and outside the family circle. The other was her frequently interrupted
formal schooling in India and in Europe. These
two main aspects are to be viewed within a larger
context of the historically conditioned circumstances
(political unrest and social upheaval) of India in
the pre-Independence period.

Indira's beloved "Dadu," Motilal Nehru, a successful lawyer with substantial professional income,
had modern but bourgeoise ideas about upbringing
and education. He believed in engaging gover-
nesses and sending his grandchildren to exclusive
and expensive boarding schools run by European
Missionaries for the children of the upper class
Indians. But these ideas were countered and cor-
rected by Jawaharlal's anxious desire as a convinced socialist to let Indira grow up in a more
middle-class atmosphere. Motilal, a patriarch in
the classical tradition, had the desire and capacity
to give his children and grandchildren the best of
everything—housing, education and a home atmosphere pervaded with enlightened solicitude and af-

fection. He was the leader of the Opposition during the period of pre-Independence. On April 8, 1929— when two revolutionaries, Bhagat Singh and Batukeswar Dutt, threw a bomb at the Treasury Benches, then occupied by the British and a few Indian members of the Viceroy's Council, in order "not to kill but to make the deaf hear" — Motilal Nehru alone remained calm and unruffled and did not get up from his seat amidst all the excitement and panic. He was one of those few men who could laugh in the face of a lot of trouble. The granddaughter admired the old gentleman immensely.

Indira once said that in the earliest years of her life, the influence of her grandfather's personality was even greater than that of her father. "I admired grandfather as a strong person, and I loved the tremendous zest for life which he had and which my father also developed later on; but I was tremendously impressed with my grandfather's bigness — I don't mean physically — but, you know, he seemed to embrace the whole world. I loved the way he laughed."

However, another individual who exercised great influence on Indira's character and outlook was the Father of the Nation, Mahatma Gandhi. It was he who shattered all the worldly ambitions of the Nehru clan and brought them down from the marble towers of luxury to the mud huts of humility and simplicity. It was he who constrained them to leave their proud professions and devote their lives as the servants of the masses. More has been written and said about this man than any other individual **of the twentieth** century, and deservedly so, for he exercised more influence on his fellowmen than any other leader of the century.

Indira has no clear recollection as to when she first met Mahatma Gandhi. "I cannot remember any time when he was not there, a part of my life and my consciousness." Whenever he came to Allahabad, Mahatma stayed in Anand Bhawan and, with his well-known love of children, he was irresistibly drawn to Indira, who was still kicking her little toes in the cradle. It was at the age of four that Indira, with all the women folk of the Nehru family (for Motilal and Jawaharlal were sentenced), made her first pilgrimage to Mahatma Gandhi's *Ashram* at Sabarmati near Ahmedabad where the annual Congress session was being held. For Indira the Ashram routine was the first taste of austerity and discipline: "waking up at 4 a.m., assembling for prayers on the banks of the Sabarmati, partaking of simple but tasteless meals, sleeping on the floor, cleaning places and washing floors." There is no evidence that Indira resented or revolted against the rigors of the Ashram life. There is evidence that although she had been crying her eyes out for her grandfather and father, Indira was strangely soothed and pacified by the gentle and affectionate solicitude of the Mahatma. He had reached her heart and made her respect the dignity of labor.

About ten years later, in 1932, Gandhi undertook a "fast-unto-death" as a protest against the separate electorates given by Ramsay Macdonald's Communal Award to the "Depressed Classes." Jawaharlal's first reaction was to feel "annoyed with him for choosing a side issue for his final sacrifice," and he "felt angry with him at his religious and sentimental approach" to a political question; also he was angry with the people of India whose social backwardness precipitated such a crisis which might take Gandhi's life. In such a conflicting psychological state he wrote to Indira, who was at the Poona school: "If Bapu died? What would India be like then? . . . Oh, India is a horrid country to allow her great men to die; and the people of India are slaves and have the minds of slaves to bicker and quarrel about trivial things and forget freedom itself."

But Gandhi's felt-in-judgment of the situation proved to be the right one, and Jawaharlal wrote again to Indira: "News came of the tremendous upheaval all over the country, a magic wave of enthusiasm running through Hindu society, and untouchability appeared to be doomed. What a magician, I thought, was this little man sitting in Yervada Prison, and how well he knew how to pull the strings that move people's hearts." By that time Indira's heart strings were already "pulled" and her own contribution already started. Indeed, having received her father's letter (If Bapu died? . . ."), she took leave from the school and, along with her cousin sisters, she went to call on the fasting "Bapu" in Yervada Prison, not far from the Poona school. Then she became action-oriented in order to bring about a "change of heart" within her school environment. Along with her teacher Mrs. Vakil, Indira observed one day's fast, then she wrote an essay on the need for removal of untouchability and

spoke in the same lines at a meeting held to pray
for the Mahatma's life. "What Bapu needs," she
said, "are not our prayers but our action. We must
do something to save him." Next morning she
"adopted" the little daughter of the school sweeper
woman, gave her a bath and thorough scrubbing,
oiled and combed her hair, dressed her in clean and
new clothes which she had bought for the child
out of her pocket money and let the daughter of the
"untouchable" sleep next to her at night. After
doing all this for "Bapu," Indira felt a strange
peace of fulfillment and profound conviction which
would lead her later to the rational idea of the
Union of India as a "nation" in the making and as
a unity in multiplicity apart from historically-con-
ditioned barriers of languages and castes.

The other personal influences are to be viewed
in terms of Indira's frequently interrupted formal
schooling. "I changed schools so many times that
it is difficult to keep track of all of them." These
changes were to a large extent explained by her
father's frequent terms of imprisonment, her mother's recurring illnesses, eventually developing into
a chronic case of tuberculosis, and the consequent
unsettled family life.

Indira was sent to one school after another: a
kindergarten in Delhi, a convent school in Allahabad
at the age of six, the "Pupil's Own School" in Poona in 1932-34, Tagore's special institute in Shantiniketan in 1934-35, an unfinished school year at
Bex (Switzerland) in 1935-36, and Summerville
College at Oxford in 1936-41. Her stay at Oxford
was interrupted for about one year by a severe at-

tack of pleurisy and consequent admission to a sanatorium at Leysin, in Switzerland, in 1938-39. This interrupted schooling was integrated by her father's library (Indira read widely and even precociously) and by her father's acting as a teacher, preacher, guide, correspondent and philosopher.

In 1931, Nehru, while in prison, started a correspondence course in world history for Indira. The character of these letters was rather polemical and partial, yet of great artistic value. These personal letters were later compiled in two volumes under the title of *Glimpses of World History*. The *Glimpses* formed the basis of Indira's political thinking.

As a teacher, Nehru suggested to his daughter good books and the way to study them. His New Year's gifts were invariably books, such as those by H. G. Wells, Julian Huxley and G. P. Wells.

Once in a while he conveyed to her some inspiring thoughts from his own readings. In one of his letters, the father reminded the daughter of George Bernard Shaw's interpretation of the true joy of life as ''being thoroughly worn out before you are thrown on the scrap heap; the being a force of nature, instead of a feverish, selfish little clod of ailments and grievances, complaining that the world will not devote itself to making you happy.''

Nehru was anxious to arrange a formal education for Indira. He had heard about a little private boarding school started by Mr. and Mrs. Koonverbai Jehangir Vakil, a nationalist-minded Parsi couple whose concept of education corresponded with Nehru's. Therefore, since Gandhi had decreed that Indira ought to go to school and not to jail, she was sent off to Poona to join the "Pupil's Own School" (1932-34). English and history were her strong points. She was very good in mathematics; French came easily to her and she was far ahead in literature. Unlike most of her fellow students, she regularly read the daily newspaper, and the subjects of her essay writing were invariably political. The students had a mock parliament and when the annual elections came around, Indira was unanimously elected "Prime Minister." Besides, she was the Secretary of the school Literary Society and, despite her innate shyness (according to Indira, her father, too, was shy: "not aloof, as so many believed, but shy by nature, and he remained so till the last years of life"), she could express herself quite well in debates, provided the subject under discussion strongly interested her.

She overcame her shyness when she took part in amateur dramatics: in Tagore's *Ritu Raj* (Cycle of Spring) and in *Bhaino Bhed* (Gujarati adaptation of an English play). She took active part in the school sports and games (such as the vigorous *"hututu"* or *"Kabaddi"*), liked to go on picnics, excursions and cross-country hikes. But, her favorite pastime was hill climbing (like Nehru's). She learned to twine the "lathi" and excelled in lezim rhythmic drill. Being older than the other girls, Indira took almost a motherly interest in her younger classmates (dressing them, combing their hair and helping them with their lessons). As Mrs. Vakil says: "They all looked up to Indira *'Didi'*. She was a good organizer, and had an or-

ganizing temperament.'' All games and sports, picnics and excursions, debates and meetings were invariably organized by Indira. But in the night,
after lights had been put out, the girls in her room
would hear Indira softly crying in bed. Her father
in prison and her mother either in prison or on
her sickbed would be the reasons for her sobbing.
For the *Glimpses* letters would come in — ''We
want independence, of course. But we want something more. We must sweep away the dirt and
poverty and the misery from our country. We must
also clean up, as far as we can, the cobwebs from
the minds of so many people which prevent them
from thinking and cooperating in the great work
before us. It is a great work, and it may be that
it will require time . . . . But freedom is a goddess
hard to win; she demands, as of old, human sacrifices from her votaries.''

Indira was admitted to the seventh class in 1932,
and creditably completed the tenth class in 1934:
four classes in three years. On the last day of school,
she left for Calcutta to attend to her ailing mother.

Kamala, a deeply religious person used to the
insights of meditation and contemplation, seemed
to have some premonitions of her own death. She
and Indira would sit together for hours in the
Math (monastery) on the bank of the river Hoogli
and look at the waters as they slowly flowed to the
Bay of Bengal. Perhaps the flow of the river indicated to her the flow of life itself which ultimately
merges in the eternal spiritual source, compared
in Indian philosophy to the ocean. As the river
flows continuously by, life also continues. When

the old life vanishes, new life appears. The nearness of her reliable daughter was an evidence to
this. As we do not see where the waters come from
and where they disappear, so life's origin and end
are shrouded in mystery. It is clear from the radiance in the life of Kamala that she had found a satis-
fying philosophy of life through her study, meditation and communion with the universal soul. She
was still young, life was challenging to her, there
was much to do for the freedom struggle. Her love
to her husband and the affection for the daughter
were "in flower." She did not want to leave the
joys of companionship of the beloved. But she
knew the gravity of her illness and the inevita-
bility of her parting from these earthly ties. She
prepared her mind to leave quietly when the time
came.

When Indira passed the matriculation examination of the Bombay University, Nehru wanted to
send her to college. But he did not like the authoritative and oppressive climate of government colleges of those days. During a brief interlude out
of jail, he discussed with Rabindranath Tagore
the possibility of sending Indira to Shantiniketan
("abode of peace"). On April 27, 1934, he wrote
to Tagore's Secretary, Anil Kumar Chanda, suggesting that Indira should go there "for a year
or so at least, and perhaps for more.   I shall discuss this with her (Indira) when I see her, for,
of course, decisions must not be imposed on a modern girl." As for subjects, she "may choose them
after she goes there." Indira did agree, and she

was admitted to the First Year Class in the Arts
course at the beginning of the new academic
session in July, 1934.

Shantiniketan is a beautiful countryside with a
peaceful atmosphere near Calcutta. Tagore, the Nobel Prize winning poet, had been striving to revive
India's cultural heritage. Talented writers, musi-
cians and artists had been attracted to Shantiniketan's cultural center to give their service to the
youth. Daily life there was based upon simplicity,
austerity (like Gandhi's *Ashram*), beauty and efficiency. Tagore wanted the young people (most
of whom came from well-to-do families) to experience and understand the rigors of life as experienced
by the masses of India (in Gandhi's spirit), but
at the same time in the unified vision of the fields
of art (in Tagore's own spirit). All students were
trained in self-help. They had to get up at 4:30
a.m., make their own beds, get breakfast, attend
classes at 6:00 a.m., and so on. Boys and girls
had their own chores in these self-help activities. Indira — who arrived barefoot and dressed in a coarse
khadar sari at the great surprise of the students
(who had imagined that she would have come in
high heeled shoes and in a French chiffon sari) — immediately adapted herself to this order of austerity.

Mrs. Asoka Sinha, a roommate of Indira, remem-
bers Indira at Shantiniketan as "shy, sober but
lively, and interested in everything." Reserved and
serious during the study hours, she relaxed among
her classmates and hostel friends. Apart from
regular classes, she wanted to learn painting, singing and dancing. She spent much time in the *Kala*

Bhawan (Art Center). She would often go to Tagore's studio and sit in a corner, quietly watching the great man at work on his paintings. Indira regards Tagore's influence as one of the most important and abiding influences in her life. "I was greatly influenced by Tagore. With police always coming in to arrest my parents, there was insecurity at home. I felt in Tagore a peaceful atmosphere. Thanks to my father, I was already familiar with world literature, but it was only when I went to Shantiniketan that Tagore opened for me the fascinating world of art. I had always regarded poetry as something separate from life. Tagore showed that all the arts were integrated. Before I went to Shantiniketan, I had not heard much about music or seen much painting and dancing."

Jawaharlal had already finished his *Glimpses* letters by then. In the "Last Letter" of that series he had written: "You must not take what I have written in these letters as the final authority on any subject. A politician wants to have a say on every subject, and he always pretends to know much more than he actually does. He has to be watched carefully " He had ended the letter and the series with a direct quotation from Tagore's *Gitanjali* (Song Offering), the poem which received the Nobel Prize in 1913:

"Where the mind is without fear and the head
    is held high;
Where knowledge is free;
Where the world has not been broken up into
    fragments by narrow domestic walls;
Where the mind is led forward by Thee into

ever-widening thought and action —
Into that heaven of freedom, my father, let
my country awake!

Indira marvelled at the strange synthesis of
thought between Tagore, the sage and philosopher,
and her father, the revolutionary and the man of
action. She perceived in Tagore a potential revolutionary and man of action, and in her father a
potential sage and philosopher.

Tagore's favorite dance form was Manipuri dancing: "light, gay, and full of warmth and sunshine,
a thing of joy and beauty and supremely adaptable
to group dancing." He was going to take Indira
in his troupe which was going on a tour of India.
In the rehearsal hall of the Art Center, Indira was
going over the intricate gestures and delicate movements of the Manipuri. Being a perfectionist, she
was a little apprehensive but she was confident, too,
for her limbs had become attuned to the subtle
rhythms of the dance after a year of discipline
and practice. Suddenly there came a messenger:
"Gurudev (Tagore) wants to see you immediately."
She reported immediately to Tagore's studio. He
showed her the telegram from her father in prison.
Kamala was seriously ill, and he requested that Indira be sent off to Allahabad immediately to look
after her mother with the implied meaning of accompanying her mother to Europe. Indira bore
the shock with equanimity and courage. She went
around, bidding farewell to her friends, and then
politely declined Tagore's suggestion that one of
the professors accompany her to Allahabad. "My
father has trained me to travel alone," she said

with a quiet determination and, taking leave of Tagore, she left alone for Allahabad.

When she left Shantiniketan, Tagore wrote to her father on April 20, 1935: "It is with a heavy heart I bade farewell to Indira, for she was such an asset to our place. I have watched her very closely and felt admiration for the way you have brought her up. She has your strength of character as well as your ideas. Her teachers, all in one voice, praise her and I know she is extremely popular with the students." And Indira would one day tell her father: "I was glad of my stay at Shantiniketan — chiefly because of Gurudev. In the very atmosphere there his spirit seemed to roam and hover over one and follow one with a loving though deep watchfulness. And his spirit, I feel, has greatly influenced my life and thought."

Tagore has been called a universal man. He was a scholar who had understanding and appreciation for world literature. As an artist he harmonized in his personality the cultures of mankind. He was a religious man who accepted the good in all the faiths of mankind. In his aspiration for youth, he wanted them to have an integrated understanding of the world of the arts. Thus, he developed the various arts in Shantiniketan and gave students an opportunity to learn and to participate in them. As part of his program to promote interreligious understanding he arranged the observance of Christmas, Holi and various other festivals. At a Christmas celebration at the University, Tagore spoke of Christ as one who had never set foot on the soil of India but exercised more influence than any other religious leader. In programs of this nature the poet tried to develop interreligious understanding and intercultural harmony. An atmosphere of this nature was most enriching for the teenager whom her father had already prepared for a world view by his *Glimpses of World History*.

Indira, after leaving school at Shantiniketan, spent anxious days by the side of her ailing mother. These days of anxiety stretched into weeks of agony. Her father, who had been in prison for the past six months, was suddenly released because of the deteriorating condition of his wife. On the night of August 11, 1934, Nehru was sent from Dehra Dun Jail under police escort to Allahabad. The next evening he reached Prayag Station in Allahabad. There he was informed by the district magistrate that he was being released only temporarily to enable him to visit his ailing wife. Thus, he arrived at Anand Bhawan to greet his wife and daughter. The days were filled with many friends continually coming to see Nehru and inquire after Kamala's health. For the father and daughter there were home comforts and better food. However, anxiety for Kamala's health cast a thick shadow over the atmosphere. In his autobiography, Jawaharlal describes Kamala's condition with moving pathos. "There she lay, frail and utterly weak, a shadow, a shadow of herself, struggling feebly with her illness, and the thought that she might leave me became intolerable." Nehru, the dynamic activist, capable of doing so much, grieved over his inability to be of help to his beloved in her hour of greatest need. He continued in his reflective mood to say that after eighteen years, Kamala had still retained her "girlish and virginal appearance" and that there was nothing matronly about her.

Nehru, himself, having been through intense political struggles and long terms of imprisonment, was visibly aged. He was partly bald, his hair was gray and deep lines crossed his face. Cobwebs gathered under his sunken eyes. Often when Nehru went out with Kamala, people used to think that she was his daughter; indeed, Kamala and Indira looked like two very lovely sisters. Sometimes the confusion became more confounded when Indira, who by now had grown in girth, was taken for the mother of the very thin Kamala. Jawaharlal stated with chagrin that this had happened many times!

On August 23, the eleventh day after his release, a police car drove up to Anand Bhawan. The officer went to Jawaharlal and said in his cryptic manner that his time was up and he must go with him to Naini Prison. Kamala had gone upstairs to get his clothes. He followed her to take leave. And then what followed may best be described in the words of Jawaharlal, "Suddenly she clung to me and, fainting, collapsed. This was unusual for her as we had trained ourselves to take this jail-going lightly and cheerfully and to make as little fuss about it as possible." It was evident that Kamala was clinging to Jawaharlal and her own life as she probably had premonitions of the nearness of parting from earthly life.

The re-arrest of Nehru seemed to have worsened Kamala's condition. Jawaharlal in his autobiography uses the following sentences from R. S. Pandit's translation of *Rajatarangini* (The River of Kings) to express the lights and shadows of his life of continuing duress. "Shadow is itself unrestrained in its path while sunshine, as an incident of its very nature, is pursued a hundred fold by nuance. Thus is sorrow from happiness a thing apart; the scope of happiness, however, is hampered by the aches and hurts of endless sorrows." After some weeks, Kamala was sent to Bhowali Hill Station. In order that he could be near Kamala, Nehru was transferred from Naini Prison to Almora District Jail in the mountains. The change of place brought some improvement.

On the advice of doctors in May 1935, Kamala was sent to Europe for further treatment. Indira accompanied her mother to the sanatorium in Badenweiler in Schwarzwald, Germany. There she kept a lonely vigil beside her emaciated mother's bedside. She felt helpless. Suffering from an advanced stage of tuberculosis, Kamala's condition deteriorated steadily. No amount of medication or nursing seemed to be of avail.

During this time a devoted family friend, Feroze Gandhi, often took leave from his studies at the London School of Economics and visited the ailing Kamala and her daughter. Fond of "Kamala Aunty" and anxious to serve the family of Jawaharlal Nehru, Feroze gallantly assisted Indira in her nursing. A strong affection developed between Indira and Feroze during this trying period; and, out of the furnace of distress, there rose a flame of love.

Despite painstaking care by Indira and Feroze

and the constant efforts of the doctors, Kamala's condition grew steadily worse. Apprehensive, Indira wired her father at the prison, informing him of her mother's grave condition.

His last five and one half months' sentence suspended on September 4, a weary and worried Nehru rushed to his wife's bedside. His arrival brought new hope and joy and a new lease of life to his wife. She showed slight improvement. For hours he sat by her side, sometimes talked to her, at other times read from new books; most of the time they communed silently. In India where they were continuously involved in the freedom struggle they rarely found time to be together. Now far from the battlefield for a while, they belonged to each other. The joy of their companionship became a healing balm.

It was not long before Nehru received the news that he had been elected to the presidency of the Indian National Congress for the second time. This greatly disturbed him. For several sleepless nights he reread his summons and thought on it. He found himself in a dilemma, not knowing what to do, or what was right to do. He had to decide either to leave Europe or resign from the Congress Presidency. He couldn't bring himself to leave Kamala. Although somewhat improved, her condition continued to be serious. She was moved from Baden-weiler to a sanatorium in Lausanne, Switzerland.

Just about this time, however, Kamala seemed to show a sudden improvement in her condition. She insisted that he must go and return after the Congress session was over. He made arrangements for travel to India. But, still the anxious husband, he did not feel at ease. He assured his beloved that he would not be gone long, two or three months at the most; and that if he was needed, a cable could have him back in a matter of days. So with these statements, he reluctantly prepared to leave.

But somehow the doctors knew better; they asked him to postpone his departure for a week or so. He immediately did so. Kamala became worse. Some changes took place within her being. She never mentioned what it was; but she seemed to lose her will to live; her mind wandered. Once she said, "Somebody's in the room with us." Just before dawn one morning, she quietly passed away. Her body was cremated to an urnful of ashes in the crematorium of Lausanne.

Thus ended a lovely life. While being gnawed away by an internal disease, she struggled even to the last to give herself so that the flame of freedom might shine brightly for ever in her motherland. Her sister-in-law, Krishna, quotes from a letter of a friend, a beautiful tribute to the treasured memory of Kamala ". . .her life was like the luminous flame of an oil lamp. It wavered, it brightened, it grew in intensity all the time and then quietly when the oil got drained the flame flickered and died."

Grief-stricken, father and daughter consoled each other. This was yet another bitter blow of death in the young life of Indira. First she lost her beloved grandfather; now she lost the one closest to her heart. She now clung to her Papu. But he had to leave shortly for India.

Nehru took the precious urn containing the ashes

of his helpmate to Allahabad by plane. On arriving home he saw the many relatives and friends who looked at him in silent sorrow.

He hastened to perform the last rites. Of these he later wrote in moving words, "We carried the precious urn to the swift-flowing Ganges and poured the ashes into the bosom of that noble river. How many of our forbears she had carried thus to the sea, how many of those who still follow us will take that last journey in the embrace of her waters." The remains of Kamala were embraced and fondly received by the river she loved. How often she has looked with admiring eyes at those waters. Perhaps as she looked at them and meditated, she saw the beyond. Apparently Jawaharlal did not have a glimpse of that beyond. He was weighed down with sorrow. The thoughts of impending war troubled him. To add to these worries were his financial difficulties. He tried to find comfort by plunging into political work in the interests of India's freedom struggle. Also, he tried to awaken his countrymen to the dangers of Nazism and Fascism. The threat of a world war was rapidly spreading throughout Europe, and Hitler's armies were preparing to march into country after country.

Indira went to London during 1936, prepared to enter Oxford. While in London she met a former classmate from Gujarat, Shanta Gandhi. They rented an apartment together in a London boarding house on Fairfax Road. This was a new experience for Indira; away from the sheltered restrictions of Shantiniketan and the protection of Anand Bhawan, she was now on her own. Her funds being limited because of her father's financial plight; she had to live very thriftily. Nevertheless she was enthusiastic about her new-found freedom. On her own at last, Indira and Shanta danced in many shows organized for the Spain Aid Committee; on one occasion Indira donated her bracelet, which was auctioned for fifteen dollars. Both worked as volunteers for the India League (which was led by Mr. V. K. Krishna Menon). When their political obligations permitted, they would attend operas and theatres.

Though far away from home she kept in close touch by means of correspondence and news media with the whirlwind changes taking place in India.

Mohammed Ali Jinnah, who had taken over the leadership of the All-India Moslem League in 1934, sponsored a scheme called Pakistan (which means land of the pure) calling for an entirely separate Moslem state. It was part of a two nation theory propounded by some scholars according to which India was to be divided into two nations, one where Hindus were in the majority and the other where Moslems were in the majority. In some respects this proposition was considered an outcome of years of the "divide and rule" policy of the British government.

The leaders of the Congress, both Hindus and Moslems, rejected the theory and campaigned for a free India where secularism would be a cornerstone of the democratic process.

In 1935, the British Parliament set up a new constitution for India and made certain changes in the Indian government in terms of the Government of India Act. This act provided for a federation which would include the princes of the Indian states as well as the governors of the provinces. The federation did not materialize because most of the princes feared they might lose some of their local authority through this form of government.

The 1935 Act created provincial legislative assemblies, elected by about eleven percent of the people (who constituted the qualified electorate). The act further provided that each governor would form his cabinet, and that all the cabinet members would be Indians. But the viceroy and the governor retained their powers of absolute veto over all legislative acts, and the central government kept most of the control of India's finances.

Under the leadership of Jawaharlal Nehru, the Congress Party campaigned vigorously in the general election. In 1937, Nehru's election campaigns were in some ways like an education campaign. He tried to inculcate in his audience a sense of national unity that transcends barriers of region, language and religion. He wanted to inspire them with the hope of a free India in which there would be a better life for the toiling millions. These travels were also for him an education, a discovery of India. He summarized his observation of the panoramic view of India in colorful scenes.

"When I think of India, I think of many things: of broad fields dotted with innumerable small villages; of towns and cities I have visited; of the magic of the rainy season which pours life into the dry parched up land and converts it suddenly into a glistening expanse of beauty and greenery, of great rivers and flowing water; of the Khyber

Pass in all its bleak surroundings; of the southern tip of India; of people individually and in the mass; and above all of the Himalayas, snow-capped, or some mountain valley in Kashmir in the spring, covered with new flowers, and with a brook bubbling and gurgling through it."

In the course of about four months Nehru traveled nearly 50,000 miles. He used every means of transportation that was available. "I traveled by airplane, railway, automobile, motor truck, horse carriages of various kinds, bullock cart, bicycle, elephant, camel, horse, steamer, paddle-boat, canoe and on foot." Ten million persons must have attended the meetings. Several millions more came in contact with him during his journeying by road.

The Indian National Congress had a landslide victory at the polls in eight provinces. As the majority party they constituted the ministries in these provinces under British governors. The Congress ministers began to work earnestly at their jobs and especially on programs such as rural reconstruction to improve the lot of the villagers. However, their projects came to an abrupt halt when, on September 3, 1939, the British government declared war against Germany and made the pronouncement that India was automatically at war with Germany. To have thus drafted India was infuriating to the Congress leaders. All the Congress ministers resigned and a program of individual satyagraha was started to protest the dictatorial procedure.

About fifteen months before the declaration of war, in June of 1938, Indira's father arrived in England for a visit. He stayed in Europe for five months. Constantly on the move, speaking, attending meetings and conferences, he was disappointed that he had so little time for his only daughter; therefore, he persuaded Indira to return with him to India before resuming her studies at Oxford. That gave Indira the spendid opportunity of spending three months at home with her ailing grandmother. The old lady was happy to have Indira by her side, for she had a notion that she might not live much longer. Then one day Indira suddenly remembered that she was twenty-one. She also remembered how nine years before, at the Congress headquarters next door in Swaraj Bhawan, she was turned down when she applied for membership in the Congress on the ground that she was too young. This time with sure steps and steady gait, she strode to the Congress office and declared, "I am twenty-one." Forthwith she was enrolled as a full member of the Congress; it was another notable milestone for the political pilgrim.

By April of 1939, Indira was back at Summerville College, Oxford. Soon afterwards there came news that her grandmother was no more, and Indira felt another link with her childhood tragically snapped. She remembered how once — still at the Poona school — she had been proudly distressed to read that her grandmother, while leading a procession, had been badly beaten by the Police in a lathi charge. She had been knocked down, repeatedly hit on the head with clubs, and, with blood oozing from an open head-wound, she had lain unconscious on the roadside till someone picked her up and took her home in a car. Yet, in writing to

Indira, she had only casually mentioned the incident, saying how happy she was to share "with our volunteer boys and girls the privilege of receiving cane and lathi blows."

Then came World War II and the launching of the Individual *Satyagraha* in India. Nehru once again was back in prison. A single thought kept hammering in Indira's mind: "I must go back, go back, go back." For she was now a fullfledged member of the Congress, entitled to offer *satyagraha* and court arrest. She remembered how profoundly she had been inspired as a child by the tale of the martyrdom of Joan of Arc, how she had replied to a question of her teacher at Allahabad that "I would like to be someone like the Joan of Arc." Also, she remembered her father's letter of November 30, 1930, on her thirteenth birthday: ". . . My presents cannot be very material or solid. They can only be of the air and of the mind and the spirit, such as a good fairy might have bestowed on you — things that even the high walls of prison cannot stop . . . do you remember how fascinated you were when you first read the story of Jeanne d'Arc, and how your ambition was to be something like her?"

But Indira, already in indifferent health, came down with pleurisy. She had gone on a hike in Penn Village in the woods. The weather was cold and she was caught in a heavy rainfall and thoroughly drenched. On her return she was so ill that she was admitted to a hospital; her ailment was diagnosed as pleurisy. On instructions from her father she was rushed to a sanatorium in Switzerland.

There she remained for almost one year. In 1940, she decided to return to India. Nehru's reply was characteristic: "I am glad Indu has decided to return. There are all manner of risks and dangers, of course, but it is better to face them than to feel isolated and miserable. If she wants to return, she must do so and take the consequences." This message was sent to Indira through Nehru's sister, Mrs. Krishna Hutheesing.

Therefore, in 1941, Indira and Feroze Gandhi sailed to India in a steamer via the Cape of Good Hope. Indira thus terminated her schooling without a formal degree. She had been too deeply involved in India's political unrest and social upheaval since her childhood. Tagore's educational centre meant for her an "abode of peace" in a double sense: in a literal sense (security from police) and in a spiritual sense (a quasi "poetic vision" of the synthetic unity of all fields of art). It is to be regretted that Indira could not find another "abode of peace" for her systematic and interconnected studies at Oxford: the clash between one's own character and contrasting events in world politics and history may sometime go beyond individual human predicaments.

The long journey to India by the sea route was taken with great caution. The waters were infested with German submarines in search of allied shipping. The ship was constantly on the alert for enemy submarines.

Disembarking in South Africa, Indira was warmly welcomed by the local Indian community. Called upon to speak, she felt too shy to make speeches.

"I cannot speak and I will not speak," she said. This was her way of confronting a task for which she was not prepared mentally or temperamentally.

While sight-seeing in Durban, she had her first encounter with "apartheid." She was horrified by the slum conditions in which colored people were forced to live. Seething with fury, and full of fire, she went to the meeting and insisted on speaking. She had a subject, a flaming message, and she gave it to them. It was a shock treatment to the Indian community of merchants, traders and government servants when she denounced "apartheid" in no uncertain terms. She compared it with Hitler's persecution of the Jews. Her countrymen were roundly chastised for their abetment. They had expected sweet talk from Panditji's daughter but not this bitter brew. After that, Indira recalls: "Though we stayed for some days, there were no more invitations for us." They did not want to stir up the "hornet's nest" anymore. Her mission accomplished, Indira was able to see the sights undisturbed.

The speech in Durban was, perhaps, the decisive turning point in Indira's political and psychological development. Basically she was shy, reserved and aloof, even an introvert; but, by life-long training, she was conditioned to react and respond to the challenge of the situation with all the strength of her personality. That day, unexpectedly, she discovered herself. Henceforth, she would no more be afraid to speak to an audience, if there was something important and worthwhile to be said. Returning to India, she found plenty to speak about with all her heart and strength, and she quickly plunged into the freedom struggle. (As for her speaking, she moves her audience best when she speaks extempore, like her father.)

Chapter IV

WEDDING AND PRISON BARS

On her return to India from Europe in 1941, Indira became involved in the independence movement. Also, plans were underway for her marriage to Feroze Gandhi, a Parsee (belonging to the Zoroastrian faith) and long-time friend of the Nehru family.

Feroze was born in Bombay in 1912. His family home was in Allahabad, not far from Anand Bhawan, and as a youngster he was Indira's playmate. Under the influence of Motilal Nehru, young Feroze joined the freedom struggle. He devoted most of his time to working for the Congress Party. A very thoughtful and affectionate young man, he had helped Indira care for her ailing mother. He was especially helpful when she was being treated in Switzerland. In the words of Gandhi, "He (Feroze) nursed Kamala Nehru in her sickness. He was like a son to her. A natural intimacy grew up between them (Feroze and Indira)." Also, he was at Kamala's bedside when she expired.

Feroze studied at the London School of Economics, where he received a Bachelor of Science Degree. He attended the Inner Temple for a time but did not stay long enough to qualify as a barrister-

at-law. With great earnestness he kept company
with Indira during her stay there. Together they
worked for the programs of the India League headed
by Mr. V.K. Krishna Menon. In 1941, Feroze and
Indira decided to return to India together.

Opposition soon mounted against the proposed
marriage of Feroze and Indira because they belonged to different faiths. Nehru, himself, wondered
whether or not, in view of their different backgrounds, they would be able to adjust well to each
other. Also, he was not sure of Feroze's ability
to provide for his daughter. Although concerned,
he recognized that his daughter was above the age
of consent and had sense enough to make up her
own mind on such matters. He was not given to
imposing his will on her and he had great consider-
ation for her independence. As a matter of fact,
he had from childhood days encouraged her to
stand on her own feet.

Nehru and Mahatma Gandhi received many written and oral protests from various religious organizations and individual fanatics. Some of these
communications were nasty; others were threatening.
Many letters reached Indira, some of which were
threatening letters. Others were plainly abusive.
Concerning these, Indira said later without bitterness that "the entire Indian Nation disapproved."
As there appeared to be a lot of fuss and fury,
Nehru issued a statement on February 26, to assuage
the excitement. "I have long held the view," he
stated, "that though parents may and should advise
in the matter, the choice and ultimate decision must
be with the two parties concerned. That decision

if arrived at after mature deliberation must be given effect to, and it is no business of parents or others to come in the way. When I was assured that Indira and Feroze wanted to marry one another I accepted willingly their decision and told them that it had my blessing.''

As usual, the family friend, Mahatma Gandhi, was consulted. In a letter written from his head-quarters in Wardha, on March 4, 1942, the following instructions were given: ''About Indira's marriage, I hold a firm opinion that none from outside need to be invited. A few persons who are at Allahabad may, however, be called as witnesses. You can send invitations (*Lagna Patrika*) to as many people as you like. Ask for blessings from everybody, but no one in particular need take the trouble of coming. If any person is asked to come, no one can be left out. It has to be considered whether Indira likes to go to this extent of simplicity or not.''

The wedding took place on Thursday, March 26, 1942. The day was auspicious according to Hindu religion because the festival celebrating the start of spring (*Vasanta Panchami*) was held on that date. The day was bright and sunny in Allahabad. A gentle breeze played with the flowers that decorated the mantle at Anand Bhawan. It was springtime and all the flowers were in bloom to greet the new bride and bridegroom. The air was fragrant with the perfume-laden blossoms of roses, marigolds and jasmines.

Indira's wedding gown was a pink sari edged with embroidered silver flowers which had been woven with loving care from the fine cotton yarn (spun while in jail) of her father. Traditionally, an Indian bride wore peach, pink or red for the ceremony, as white was the color of mourning and was worn only by widows. It is customary for all Indian brides to be waited on by her friends, and several of Indira's friends were present to assist her. Her hair was brushed with fragrant oil until it glistened. Her sari was gently draped around her and she was bedecked with bracelets, necklace and other ornaments, all made of fresh leaves and flowers. Her dressing complete, she greeted her friends. She had never looked more beautiful. The scented oils brought out the delicate texture of her skin, and the pink sari enhanced her fragile beauty.

Relatives and friends had been arriving for two or three days and Anand Bhawan had acquired a festive air. Gifts had been pouring in for weeks and they were still streaming into the bridal chamber. Indira, flushed and happy, but trying to remain calm in spite of her mounting excitement, was accepting congratulations from relatives and friends.

Her aunt, Krishna Hutheesing, recalls in her famous autobiography, *With No Regrets,* that "she looked lovelier than ever, frail and almost ethereal." She laughed and talked to those around her "but sometimes her big black eyes would darken and hold a distant sorrowful look. What dark cloud could mar the joy of this happy day? Was it a longing for the young mother who was no more? ... Or was it the thought of parting from the father, a father whose very life she had been? She was leaving him now to a life that would be lonelier for him than it had ever been before."

The wedding took place in an open veranda of
the home. There was a *mandup* (a canopied square
erected for the occasion) set up; and there was a
tiny enclosure for the lighting of the sacrificial fire.
Two mats were laid on one side for Indira and
Feroze and two mats on the other side for Indira's
parents. There were carpets spread around for the
invited guests. The uninvited guests were not turned
away. Some of these uninvited guests even sat on
branches of nearby trees to see the wedding.

The ceremony started with Indira's giving her consent to the marriage. The ceremony that symbolized
the determination to preserve freedom and the love
of freedom — the *Jaya-Homa* (a sacrifice to victory) — was next. The Sanskrit sloka was recited by
Indira.

The second part of the marriage ceremony began with Nehru giving away his daughter (the *Kan-
ya Dan*). After this Indira got up from her father's
side and sat beside Feroze. Feroze recited a *sloka*
(verse) promising to act in accordance with Indira's
wishes and to never neglect her.

The *Homa* was next. During this stage of the
ceremony the sacrificial fire was lit and clarified butter was poured into it with a ladle of silver by the
chanting priests. The crucial *Sapta-Padi* was performed next. The couple walked around the fire
seven times hand in hand. This set the seal on the
wedding. A symbolic meal was eaten by Feroze and
Indira out of each other's hands. Then flower petals
were showered (the *Posh-Puja*) on Feroze and Indira by the ladies of the house while marriage songs
enhanced the occasion. Indira and Feroze stood be-

fore the guests and the priests and recited the *verses* from the *Rig Veda;* the ceremony was thus concluded.

After the ceremony everyone was caught up in the wedding festivities. Indira and Feroze, whose childhood friendship had blossomed into love, were now united in marriage, "to have and to hold until death do part."

The newly-weds went on a honeymoon to Kashmir, the world-renowned vacation resort. It has been called a "house of many stories" because of its terraced landscape. Nestled beneath the towering Himalayan Mountains, it presents a beautiful and picturesque view from above, spreading out like a lush green carpet in the valley below. Man-made canals link the blue waters of the rivers and lakes, and great Chinar trees provide shade from the sun. Its cool mountain climate offers an ideal escape from the scorching summer heat of the plains. It is a dreamland for honeymooners.

Indira and Feroze had very happy days in the cool valley of Kashmir, abounding with the beauties of spring. Meanwhile, Nehru was in the scorching heat of Allahabad preparing the country for an all-out struggle for independence. On the lighter side he received a telegram from his daughter and son-in-law in Kashmir: "Wish we could send you some cool breezes from here." With characteristic humor, finding good even in adversity, Nehru replied: "Thanks — But you have no mangoes." (Summer in Allahabad was the season for the delicious mango fruit which Indira relished so much.)

Upon returning to Allahabad, Indira and Feroze

lived in a small rented house at 4 Fort Road not far from Anand Bhawan. They began to work in earnest with the freedom movement. The students of the Ewing Christian College decided to hoist the national tri-color in the college compound. Indira was invited and went there preparing to be arrested. She was horrified at the merciless beatings the students were receiving at the hands of the police as they tried to hoist the flag. Some were bleeding profusely.

The flag fell to the ground, and before the police could trample it, Indira ran and picked it up. She held the flag aloft, and the students rallied at the sight of the daughter of Nehru holding the national flag; they sang lustily. As she held the flag she felt a heavy blow on her back. The stinging pain shot through her entire body, but she did not waver. The second blow was aimed at her hand and she almost let go of the flagpole. Suddenly, she remembered that her father had been beaten and also trampled by the police. The thought of her father gave her renewed courage. She silently spoke to herself, "I will not cry and I will not let go of the flag." A violent punch threw her to the ground, and the heavy nailed boots of a policeman walked on her frail, prostrate form!

Bruised and weary, but nevertheless feeling victorious, Indira returned home. Reporting to Feroze later that night, she proudly related that, "there was a little scuffle, but, it went off well; we did hoist the flag." Her face was calm as usual. But Feroze, who was familiar with the storms behind that calm face, realized that there was more than "a little scuffle" to that flag hoisting. He reserved his comments but was greatly shocked when he learned the details. Indira had pains, but she never let a soul know about them. For information's sake, a lathi is a bamboo stick about five feet long with a lead tip. Lathi blows on one's back and hand were not friendly strokes!

Soon after the outbreak of World War II, India asked for its independence in return for its aid in the conflict. In response, the British Government sent the very personable Sir Stafford Cripps to solve the problem with a plan known as the Cripps Proposal. It was on a "take it or leave it" basis. The plan provided that India should be admitted to full dominion status following the war and be made part of the British Commonwealth of Nations. Elected delegates from the provinces of British India and appointed delegates from Indian states ruled by princes were to draw up a constitution for a Federated Dominion of India. Any state or province had the right to remain outside the Federation and make its own treaty with Britain. The British Government was to retain power during the war and to be responsible for India's defense and international relations.

The Cripps Proposal was rejected by all Indian parties because they felt it did not grant India a proper share of responsibility for its administration and defense. The Moslem League thought that the plan was too vague to satisfy its demand for the partition of India.

The failure of the Cripps mission caused a wave of indignation in India. Mahatma Gandhi called for non-violent non-cooperation. He called for the British to "Quit India."

Indira and Feroze went to Bombay for the historic All-India Congress Committee meeting held at Gowalia Tank Maidan. The Congress was engaged in an all-out effort to free India from British rule. The radicals and progressive groups were clamoring for action. The "Quit India" resolution was passed on August 8, 1942. But, before the committee could gather their resources together, a wholesale arrest of all Congress leaders was ordered.

Indira, residing with her aunt, Krishna Hutheesing, was assisting her father with his packing when the police arrived before dawn. She fled to Anand Bhawan the next day. There the Police arrived early the following morning and arrested her aunt, Vijayalakshmi Pandit. Flooded with memories of past arrests, Indira recalled the numerous times in the past when she tearfully bade farewell to her father as the police took him to prison. She was a child then, helplessly looking on, but unable to act. Now she was a child no longer. She was an adult and a respected member of Congress. She would no longer be a helpless spectator. As she gathered her three younger cousins Chandralekha, Nayantara and Tara around her, she realized she was the oldest member of the family left in Anand Bhawan. A new sense of responsibility and maturity awoke in her.

During this time, Indira became anxious about Feroze. He had been doing propaganda and other work for the Quit India Movement. As he was one of the active campaigners, a warrant for his arrest had been sent out and he had gone underground "to continue the struggle." He disguised himself by growing a beard and dressing in khakis. Because of his fair complexion and ruddy cheeks, he could easily pass as an Anglo-Indian soldier. While journeying by train from Bombay to Allahabad, he got off at a small wayside station thinking that, since he was a familiar figure in Allahabad, he might be recognized in spite of the disguise. He could not find any means of conveyance to continue his journey and became impatient. There soon appeared an army truck carrying British and Anglo-Indian soldiers. He hitched a ride on the army truck! He found the soldiers scared. They almost refused to let him get off at Allahabad saying that "The damned natives would hack him to pieces if they found him alone and unarmed!" He talked fast and convinced them that he would make out all right. So, they reluctantly let him out.

Once in Allahabad, he contacted Indira. They managed to meet secretly at night in the houses of different non-political friends. Although it was almost impossible for underground workers to get together because of the tight security measures of the police and military, Indira was able to pass on money and political literature to the workers through her husband.

Swaraj Bhawan, the Congress headquarters next door, was occupied by the military. Thus, Indira and other members had the disagreeable sight of a row of guns aimed at them across the garden wall. The servants, mostly villagers, were frightened. Every time they approached the wall they were startled by the sentry's order: "Halt! Who goes there?" Naturally, they found it difficult to reply.

Lal Bahadur Shastri had long been associated with Anand Bhawan, as he was working in close association with Nehru in the Congress Party. It was known that there was a warrant for Shastri's arrest. The sagacious Shastri assumed that no one would think that he could be so careless as to continue to stay at Anand Bhawan. So he outwitted his adversaries by doing just that. Thus, he managed to remain incognito for a while and saved greatly needed time to make arrangements for the work of the Quit India Movement to continue. He would stay within his room all day and step out for a while when it was dark. Indira would take food to him in his room. Everything had to be done cautiously without drawing the attention of outsiders. Therefore, Indira and other members of the house pretended that there was an ailing relative in the house who had to be fed and nursed in his own room. It was clear to both Shastri and his "relatives" that they could not long maintain the secrecy. The house was being watched round the clock by the police and plain clothesmen. Also, there was always the impending danger of a house search. All these considerations induced Shastri to leave the place for another hideout. But the wily plain clothesmen got the better of the shrewd Shastri. He was arrested shortly thereafter and taken to jail. Shastri had always been a helpful friend to Indira and was greatly missed at Anand Bhawan. Even as a young child, Indira had appreciated his friendliness. It is said that of all the serious faced workers of the freedom movement who frequented Anand Bhawan, he was the only person who took time out to play with the lonesome Indira.

About this time, Indira received information from reliable sources that she would soon be arrested. Thus far she had tried to remain inconspicuous; she had political chores to attend to and did not want to be locked up. But it was clear now that she would soon be behind prison bars. However, she did some quick thinking and decided to use her freedom for one more effort to arouse the people for the continuance of the freedom struggle. She hastily packed some clothes and books and went to stay elsewhere. Announcement was given by word of mouth that a public meeting would be held at five p.m. that afternoon.

Police roamed all over the city and made inquiries; they were in the dark as to the whereabouts of the meeting. They were nervous since there was so much hush-hush about the program. Crowds had gathered in shops, residences and cinema houses awaiting the meeting. At the stroke of five, Indira emerged and the crowds poured in from all sides. She managed to speak forcefully for nearly ten minutes. By then, truckloads of British soldiers arrived and formed a cordon around the meeting. Feroze, who was doing important work "underground," stayed away from the meeting. However, he was watching the proceedings through the shutters of a nearby first floor window. When he saw a gun barrel just a yard away pointing to Indira's head, he became anxious for her safety. Excitedly, he came charging out from the house yelling at the sergeant to shoot or to lower his gun. The sergeant caught Indira by the arms to lead her away to prison. The emotional crowd surged forward.

Some Congress women caught Indira's other arm and tried to free her from the sergeant. This resulted in a tug-of-war during which the belabored Indira thought she would be torn asunder. Her clothes were ripped and she received minor abrasions.

Soldiers won the day. They used rifle butts on the crowd. A large number of men and women, including Feroze and Indira, were arrested. They were taken to Naini Prison. "The ride to the jail," says Indira, "was an extraordinary one, for police in my van were apparently so moved by my talking to them that they apologized, put their turbans at my feet and wept sorrowfully because of what their job compelled them to do!"

The prisoners were huddled together in small groups, talking, when the prison matron entered and loudly announced that "Mrs. Indira is here!" Excitement surged through the barracks. As Indira entered, a hushed silence followed. Holding herself proudly, Indira was greeted warmly by the groups. She was elated to see her aunt, Vijayalakshmi Pandit, among the prisoners. Overcome with joy, they talked together long into the night.

It was only a few days later when another member of the family joined them. Mrs. Pandit's daughter, Lekha, was put in the barrack. Mrs. Pandit, keeping a diary of their stay in prison, recalls that Indira remained her same cheerful self. She was a source of inspiration to the other women prisoners. However, Indira's own words reveal how much she suffered inwardly, in spite of all her efforts to be cheerful and helpful.

"What a world of difference there is between hearing and seeing from the outside and the actual experience. No one who has not been in prison for any length of time can even visualize the numbness of spirit that can creep over one when, as Oscar Wilde writes — 'each day is like a year, a year whose days are long.' When day after day is wrapped in sameness and in spite and deliberate humiliation, Pethick Lawrence said, 'The essential fact in the life of the prisoner is that he takes on a sub-human status.' Herded together like animals, devoid of dignity or privacy, debarred not only from outside company or news but from all beauty and color, softness and grace. The ground, the walls, everything around us was mud-colored, and so became our jail-washed clothes, even our food tasted gritty. Through the barred apertures we were exposed to the dust storms, the monsoon downpour and the winter cold. Others had an interview and letter once or twice a month, but not I. My husband was in the same prison. After persistent efforts, we were permitted a short interview, but soon he was transferred to another town. I kept cheerful and busy reading and teaching. I took over the entire care of a small baby whose mother I was coaching, to enable her to earn her living on her release."

Nehru, while in prison, remembered how much his daughter enjoyed eating mangoes when a child. Realizing that she had not had her favorite fruit for a long time, he wrote to a friend to send her a basket of ripe mangoes. Evidently, a basket of delicious mangoes reached the jail. Indira inferred that the Jail Superintendent and staff had a good time eating them; for he thanked her profusely for the fruits on behalf of his staff and himself. As an after-thought Indira commented that "he didn't even have the grace" to give her or her companions "even one small piece." So goes the story of the sweet mangoes; they are symbolic because this is not the first time that both seen and unseen hands robbed sweet things from her life. When her family decided to join the freedom struggle they prepared themselves for the continuing shocks of deprivation of many precious things. Their training in courage included being ready to give up even the sweetest thing in life, "life itself," when the occasion demanded it. On another occasion a package of mangoes from her father reached her safely. This time she walked around the package extending the duration of joy, then smelled, touched and fondled the mangoes before tasting the sweetness.

Indira says that after a while there was no yearning for the outside world, "for no one worth while was there." All her near and dear ones, as well as many of the freedom fighters, were behind prison bars or "underground." Besides, she and other political prisoners were confirmed in their view that they would be there for another seven years. She was determined to suffer all privations and insults smilingly, and much happened to "smile" over. For instance, when Indira's ill health caused considerable public concern, the Governor of the United Provinces sent the Civil Surgeon to treat her. After his examination, the doctor prescribed a tonic and a special diet including delicacies such as oval-

tine. But the superintendent of the jail was in-
furiated by the prescription. As soon as the doctor
left the superintendent tore up the prescription and
tossed the pieces on the floor in front of Indira.
"If you think you are getting any of this," he said,
"you are mistaken." The emaciated patient was
amazed by all this tantrum for she had not asked
for anything at all.

Once in a long while something happened which
startled the inmates from their dreary existence.
One day a plane crashed very near the jail. It
turned out to be the tragic end of a romance. It
being war time, the cantonment near the jail was
crowded with British, American and Canadian soldiers. A Canadian ace pilot was in love with the
jail superintendent's attractive daughter. As part
of his "showing off" to impress the young lady he
used to fly low over her house. One day as he was
flying over the house a wing of the plane touched
a telegraph wire and it burst into flames. Indira
and other inmates watched with alarm as the plane
was falling towards the jail. Luckily, it skirted the
jail wall and landed on a half-built bungalow nearby.

Indira has narrated another incident of a blood
curdling nature that took place one night. The wardress, Zohra, a most unpopular woman, was shrieking with fright because a large cobra was coiled
under one of the clocks which she had to punch on
her rounds. She was afraid of the poisonous snake,
yet she was afraid she might lose her job unless
she punched the clock on time. The cobra was only
a yard from the bars of Indira's jail. She was inside
the barrack and Zohra within the outer wall. The

wardress had no stick or other weapon. She kept shouting, shrieking and crying for help to the sentry outside. He, like a rusty bureaucrat, demanded a detailed description regarding the exact location of the snake, specifications of its length and breadth and so on. *"Are Kambakht"*! (O you unfortunate one) shouted Zohra. "Have I got a tailor's tape to measure it from head to tail?"

After what seemed hours of persuasion, the sentry moved to meet the emergency! He called the matron in charge who lived two furlongs away from the prison. The sleepy matron walked to the superintendent's house to awaken him. Then the superintendent and the matron went to the main office and secured the key to the women's prison. By the time they entered the enclosure to redeem the clock from the coils of the cobra, the huge reptile had slithered away to some area of the prison grounds; no one knew where. All the prisoners had gone to sleep.

Nine months later, on May 13, 1943, Indira and her aunt were released from prison with a warning to curtail their movements. Disobeying these restrictions, Mrs. Pandit was arrested again and returned to Naini Prison.

Indira, fever-ridden with influenza, returned to Anand Bhawan alone. Her husband and father were in prison. The rigors and ordeals of nine months in prison had left their marks on her.

"All things pass and so did this," wrote Indira concerning the nightmare of imprisonment. "My unexpected release was like coming suddenly out of a dark passage — I was dazzled with the rush of life, and many hues and textures, the scale of sounds and range of ideas. Just to touch and listen was a disturbing experience and it took a while to get adjusted to normal living.''

Fortunately for Indira, her husband was released from jail in August, 1943. They lived together at Anand Bhawan. After all the trials and miseries of prison, their being together at home was like waking to joyous dawn from a nightmare.

It was not long, therefore, before she was to be a mother. She wanted good care during pregnancy. So she went to Bombay (an excellent place to get medical attention) and lived with her aunt, Mrs. Krishna Hutheesing. Her first son, Rajiv Ratna, was born on August 20, 1944. Mrs. Hutheesing conveyed the good news to the proud grandfather who was in his ''other home'' — Ahmedabad Prison.

In his reply to his sister, he wrote: ''In my letter to Indu I suggested to her to ask you to get a proper horoscope made by a competent person. Such permanent records of the date and time of birth are desirable. As for the time, I suppose the proper solar time should be mentioned and not the artificial time which is being used outside now. War time is at least an hour ahead of normal time.''

At about this time, Indian resources were being put to use by the British Government and its allies. American and British air bases had been established in India after the Japanese captured the Burma Road in 1942, and supplies were flown from India to China. India based British troops waged a vigorous campaign against Japan in Burma.

By the end of 1943, India had become a huge supply base and training center for the allied armies and air forces. The Japanese invaded eastern India in March, 1944. But British, Indian and American forces drove the invaders back into Burma.

As the British government was unable to arrive at a working agreement with the Congress leadership, most of them were continued in their imprisonment. Mahatma Gandhi was detained in the Palace of the Aga Khan near Poona. The members of the Congress Working Committee, including Jawaharlal Nehru, were kept in the Ahmednagar Fort. For Nehru, this was his last term of imprisonment. It was also the longest, lasting till June 15, 1945, for a period of 1,040 days. Altogether, he had undergone imprisonment about nine times and spent a total of 3,262 days of his life in what he euphemistically called his "other home."

Indira returned to Anand Bhawan. She was joined there by her father in June, 1945. Most of the political prisoners were soon released. Feroze, who was looking for a job to earn a good living for his family, got an appointment as Managing Director of the *National Herald* in Lucknow. This was an English daily founded by Nehru in 1937. As Managing Director, Feroze did an outstanding job and by careful management made a success of the newspaper business.

Feroze and Indira lived in a small house in Hazratgunj, Lucknow. Indira often had to divide her time between Lucknow and New Delhi so that she might look after her own house and also care for her aging father.

Early in 1946, Clement Attlee, Prime Minister of Great Britain, offered complete independence to India as soon as India's leaders could agree on a form of government for a free India. From April to June, 1946, British Government leaders in India met with leaders of Indian political and religious groups in New Delhi and Simla. Representatives of the Congress Party and the Moslem League were unable to agree and the meeting ended in failure. Bloody Hindu-Muslim riots then broke out in cities like Delhi and many persons were killed.

In 1946, Mr. Nehru had established his residence in New Delhi in a four-room flat. There Indira gave birth to her second son, Sanjay, who was born prematurely. Even while she had not fully gained her normal strength, she was entrusted by Mahatma Gandhi to free the Muslims of Delhi from fear and to take steps to end the bloody riots. First she tried to get all the hooligans arrested and thus prevent riots at their source. But this effort was not successful. So she tried the method of uniting the leadership of the locality to bring their influence to bear for peace. About five hundred leaders of the various communities were brought together at a social gathering. Out of this gathering evolved a plan of action for the relief of communal tension and the promotion of harmony. All those gathered arrived at the understanding that each one in his area would convey to the people a message of harmony and work in every way possible so that distrust and bitterness would be allayed. This gathering did much to relieve the tension among the people.

In 1947, discussions on Indian independence were re-opened by the new Viceroy, Lord Louis Mountbatten. Partition of India was agreed upon as the only way to resolve the conflict. India and Pakistan were made separate dominions in the Common-wealth of Nations. India had finally achieved her long-sought for independence. However, the Indian leaders did not accept the two nation theory. They made it clear that India would be a secular state in which people of all religions would have equal rights. Nehru was appointed acting Prime Minister. At midnight of August 14, 1947, a most impressive ceremony was held in the Constituent Assembly at which an Independent India was ushered into existence. Nehru's moving message on the occasion was heard by millions throughout the country by means of the All India Radio. "Long years ago," he declared, "we made a tryst with destiny. . .and now the time comes when we shall redeem our pledge, not wholly or in full measure, but very substantially. At the stroke of the midnight hour, when the world sleeps, India will awake to life and freedom. A moment comes, which comes but rarely in history, when we step out from the old to the new, when an age ends, and when the soul of a nation, long suppressed, finds utterance. It is fitting that at this solemn moment we take the pledge of dedication to the service of India and her people and to the still larger cause of humanity. . . .Peace has been said to be indivisible. So is freedom, so is prosperity now, and so also is disaster in this one world that can no longer be split into isolated fragments."

This was a moment of triumph for India, Nehru and his daughter. Recalling this climactic experience, Indira said to an interviewer (Mr. Arnold Michaelis for *McCall Magazine*), "Well, I was so excited and proud, you know, I really thought I would burst!'' She explained further that she felt that way "because of having taken part in the struggle" and having come to the realization that the struggle was fruitful.

The peace and joy of free India was marred by communal riots. The vast hordes of Hindu and Sikh refugees who poured into Delhi from West Pakistan brought blood curdling tales of persecution at the hands of Pakistani Muslims. Mob passions were roused against the Muslim minority in Delhi. Looting, violence and arson spread. Many innocent men, women and children were murdered in the senseless wave of revenge. Gandhi, Nehru, Indira and other leaders worked hard to end this mob violence. Mahatma Gandhi, who camped in the house of industrialist G. D. Birla, conducted daily prayer meetings to exhort people to restore order and peace in the community. The writer was present at some of these prayer meetings at which songs and prayers from the different religions were used. Quotations from the Bible, the Koran, Gita and other sacred books were used at these meetings. The Lord's Prayer (the prayer that Jesus taught his disciples) was a favorite of the Mahatma. Often he closed the meetings with the people singing in Hindi a song of religious unity. It is translated thus:

> Raghupati Raghava Raja Ram
> Ram, the king of the Universe
> He who makes the sinner pure
> He who is known by various names
>   such as Ishvara and Allah
> Let his blessings be upon all.

Gandhi stressed the unity and brotherhood of people of all religions and pointed out that basically all religions attempted to point the way to God and to a good fellowship among mankind. Nehru, while living at 17 York Road, a modest three-bedroom house, helped the refugees all he could by making two bedrooms available for them and by setting up tents on the lawn of the house to accommodate more. Indira worked untiringly with her father in looking after the household and the many helpless refugees. Although it was a time of rationing, she succeeded by the most careful management to feed the household and the refugees.

Indira's tasks were not limited to the household. Time and again she joined her father in his flying visits to areas from which reports of rioting came. In their individual capacities they tried to save Muslims in danger. At one uprising, Nehru rushed into a mob of violent rioters and snatched away the sword from the hand of one of the rioters as he was going to use it against a victim. Likewise, Indira is credited with having caught a would-be-assassin hiding in a bathroom. She took his knife away from him, hauled him out and handed him over to the police.

On another occasion, Indira rushed in a jeep to where a report came that a Muslim house was surrounded by an armed mob. News had come of fresh outbreaks of violence against non-Muslims in Pakistan. So the mob in Delhi had become more angered than ever before. Indira's jeep halted near the shouting mob; the driver of the jeep sensing the danger left the jeep and ran away! Indira heard many abusive shouts aimed against her. But she moved calmly and collectedly toward the house. The mob let her go. But one rowdy insulted her by tearing away the covering on her head. Without stopping to argue with the man she went into the house, got the frightened family out and took them to the safety of her father's house.

On January 13, 1948, Mahatma Gandhi started a fast to change the hearts of the violent parties and to restore communal harmony. "I will not take nourishment," he said, "till Moslems can walk safely in the streets of Delhi. Hindus, Sikhs and Moslems must live as brothers." There was local and national concern and anxiety for the life of the aged father of Indian independence. Many fasted in sympathy. The fast evidently had a tremendous effect in calming the Hindu and Sikh community even as it produced a most grateful response from the Muslims.

Six days after the fast was begun, Gandhi received written pledges from leaders of the various communities that peace would prevail. The Mahatma broke the fast by sipping a glass of orange juice handed to him by Maulana Abul Kalam Azad. After two days Gandhi resumed his prayer meeting. A young man threw a bomb and ran to the gate. The bomb was intended for Gandhi, but he was unhurt. The young man was caught by the people and handed to the police. Hearing the news Nehru rushed to Birla House. In his talks with Gandhi, he suggested that the prayer meetings be given up for a while as his life was in danger. "No" was the answer. "Many people came," said the Mahatma, "they need me. I must not disappoint them."

In the afternoon of January 29, Indira and her son, Rajiv, along with her aunt, Krishna Hutheesing, and cousin, Nayantara, visited Gandhi. The visit was very pleasant. "Well, well," said Bapu with a twinkle in his eyes, "have all these princesses come to see me?" They all sat in the sun, which was comfortable in the cold afternoon. Their host was in a jolly mood wearing a peasant's hat from Noakhali. He asked them, "Don't I look handsome in this hat?" All had a hearty laugh. They continued their conversation for a while; then their host concluded the pleasantries by saying "you girls, all of you vanish now, otherwise people waiting outside will curse you." Reluctantly they took leave.

On January 30, at eventide, Gandhi came to the garden to start the prayer meeting. A stoutish young man in khaki dress accosted him in the traditional salutation with folded hands. Gandhi responded with folded hands. Suddenly the young man whipped out a small revolver and fired three shots at point-blank range. Two entered the chest and one the abdomen of the Mahatma. With the words "He Ram" (O God) on his lips, the apostle of non-violence fell. It is reported that as he fell he made a gesture with his hand to indicate that his assassin was forgiven. The blood that flowed from the bare chest of the frail Bapu trembled on the green grass. He was carried to his room. He was dead. As in the case of Abraham Lincoln, he "belonged to the ages."

Nehru and Patel knelt by the body and wept, and so did the onlookers. As soon as Nehru could gather himself together he spoke to the bereaved nation by All India Radio: "Friends and comrades, the light has gone out of our lives and there is darkness everywhere. I do not know what to tell you and how to say it. Our beloved leader, Bapu (father), as we called him, the Father of the Nation is no more. Perhaps I am wrong to say that. Nevertheless, we will not see him again as we have seen him for these many years. The light has gone out, I said, and yet I was wrong. For the light that shone in this country was no ordinary light. The light that illumined this country for these many years will illumine this country for many more years. ... For that light represented something more than the immediate present, it represented the living, the eternal truths. ..."

All India mourned. So did the world. Tributes flowed to Delhi from the high and the mighty as well as the poor and lowly. More was written and said about the Mahatma than any other person in the twentieth century. A most classic analysis of the life of the Mahatma was given in a few sentences, notable for insight and understanding, by Dr. E. Stanley Jones, the American Missionary who made India his adopted home. Dr. Jones had many discussions with the Mahatma on religious themes. He once said that "Gandhi was India." "Gandhiji," he wrote, "seemed very simple, and yet he was very complex. He was a meeting place of the East and West, and yet represented the soul of the East; he was an urban man who became the voice of the peasant masses; he was passive and militant, and both at one and the same time; he was the ascetic and the servant, aloof from and yet with the multitudes, with them as their servant; he was the mystical and the practical come to embodiment, the man of prayer and the man of the spinning wheel and ten thousand other practical things connected with economic redemption; he combined the Hindu and Christian in himself, a Hindu at the center of his allegiance and yet deeply christianized; he was the simple and the shrewd, the candid and the courteous; he combined the serious and the playful, a man who could shake empires and could tickle a child beneath the chin and gain a laugh and a friend; he had poise, but in the poise of retreat and aloofness; he had power to change situations by a deep identification; he was strangely humble and strangely self-assertive; and last of all, and perhaps the most important of all, he was a person who embodied a cause—the cause of India's freedom."

The death of Gandhi made Nehru feel very miserable for a long time. The shock was unexpected. It was too severe. The loss seemed irreparable. He took much of the blame on himself. Speaking before the Constituent Assembly, he gave vent to his pent-up feelings: "I have a sense of utter shame both as an individual and as head of the government of India that we should have failed to protect the greatest treasure that we possessed." He went on to point out that it was not sufficient to mourn and that the only way to render homage to the departed leader was to express determination and dedication to the great task which Gandhi undertook and which he accomplished to such a large extent.

The death of Gandhi left a great void in the life of Nehru. There was none like him to turn to.

Now he had to rely upon himself and long-time colleagues like Sardar Patel, Rafi Ahmed Kidwai, Maulana Abul Kalam Azad and Govind Ballabh Pant. Within a ten-year period, however, death snatched away these colleagues. Thus, Nehru began to rely more and more on Indira Priyadarshini for solace and help.

India became a Republic on January 26, 1950, under the Indian Constitution adopted by the Constituent Assembly in November, 1949. Symbols of British authority were replaced by those of the newborn republic.

In his capacity as acting Prime Minister, the tasks of Nehru were heavy; he also had the official duty of entertaining guests, including world leaders. In keeping with the needs of his new position he moved to more spacious quarters of the mansion on Teen Murti Marg which was formerly occupied by the British Commander-in-Chief.

Nehru was lonely and his burdens were heavy. He did the inevitable and invited Indira and her husband to live at the Prime Minister's residence. They came with their two children and were conveniently housed in the large mansion. Feroze took great pains to make sure that nothing was done to give the impression that he was exploiting his position as son-in-law of the Prime Minister.

The big house at Teen Murti Marg was always a busy place, being the residence of the Prime Minister of India and also the residence of the "idol of India," Jawaharlal Nehru. To be official hostess in the house was to Indira a job that required much tact, patience, flexibility, great care for details, good coordination, ability to make speedy arrangements and knowledge of national as well as international menus and customs. Guests came from all parts of India and the world. Among them were Mrs. Eleanor Roosevelt, Mrs. Jacqueline Kennedy, Lord and Lady Mountbatten and a host of others. Indians, themselves, proved to be a great jigsaw puzzle in their eating habits. There were meat eaters who were vegetarians on certains days of the week. There were vegetarians who ate fish or meat or both. Hindus do not eat beef, whereas Muslims do not touch pork; they do not care to even mention that name because pork is so abominable to them. In this multiplicity of combinations, Indira had to walk a tightrope trying to accommodate all and offend none. It is said that Indira inspected the menus regularly and checked assignments daily.

Open air entertainments are always difficult in the uncertain weather conditions of Delhi. One has to put up with rains, duststorms and extreme heat. On one occasion, just as guests were arriving for an open air reception, a thunderstorm broke out. It required a quick shift indoors. It is reported that at one standing party where the bearers brought along sweets, some of the guests, instead of taking a sweet piece, relieved the bearer of the whole plate. Before a fraction of the people arrived the sweets had disappeared. Indira had to do some quick thinking. She had pakoras (fritters) made instantly and served with fruits and nuts.

The matter of protocol was especially cumbersome. Indira commented thusly: "For the women especially, there is the constant battle with protocol so as not to offend even the most particular of dignitaries and yet not to stifle the human element and keep the function interesting and homely; the daily struggle with menus to suit all tastes; the intricacies of decorating a state house and so on." She functioned so graciously and ably that she received golden opinion from visiting dignitaries and journalists from around the world. Lord Pethick Lawrence spoke of her as a charming hostess who was selflessly devoted to "the highest ideals of service." After a very pleasant tour of India with her husband, the then Vice-President Lyndon Johnson, Mrs. Johnson said, "To see India, you must visit the villages. To understand India, you must read Tagore. But to know India you must have a teacher like Indira Gandhi. I was lucky because I had all three."

Chapter V

HER FATHER'S COMPANION

A question was once asked as to what the consequences would have been if Jawaharlal Nehru had had a son instead of a daughter. Indira, expressing remarkable insight, replied that probably there would have been more difficulties, because, to begin with, the son could not have remained with the father.

Asked what she would like to have been if she had had total freedom of choice, Indira replied "I would like to have been a writer." Then she added, "I would like to have done research in history, or perhaps, in anthropology, for the latter interests me even more than history. Maybe there is a touch of the primitive in me. Whatever the reason, I would like to have been an anthropologist." This interest in the subject led her to suggest to her father, and later help in organizing, the annual pageant of folk dances and the processions of tribal peoples in their colorful costumes, which is the main attraction of the Republic Day festivities in the capital. Also interested in interior decorating, Indira furnished the Teen Murti House throughout, showing remarkable talent and taste.

Settling in New Delhi, Indira and Feroze lived

first in a bungalow on York Road, then in Nehru's
spacious Teen Murti House. She was a most reliable
source of help and comfort to her father. Though
no agreement was made, it was understood from the
first to be only a temporary arrangement. Pressured
and burdened with a multitude of problems, Nehru
often put in an eighteen-hour work day; it naturally
was important to his well-being that someone should
be there to remind him to eat, and sometimes even
to rest. Only someone who understood him, loved
him and who, in turn, commanded his affection and
respect could be such a help. There was only one
such person—his daughter.

Usually, Nehru had breakfast with his family,
which then consisted of his daughter, son-in-law and
two grandchildren. After the meal, the boys left
for school and were not seen by their grandfather
until the following morning. Even this brief moment
of family interlude was often disturbed by secretaries bringing dispatches to be read or documents
to be signed.

Indira had the unenviable task of keeping intruders away and providing some privacy for her
father. Over the years, the great leader had gathered
such a vast following of friends, admirers, curiosity
seekers and plain hangers-on that it was difficult to
secure any privacy. He tolerated all manner of
intruders, including those who followed him everywhere, even to the bathroom. Many people always
gathered around him for no business, only Darshan
or sight. They could not be blamed, for Nehru was
not only pleasing to look at, in person he was a
veritable inspiration. Indira had to intervene often,

but with great care not to offend. She knew only too well that in politics one has to tread softly so that he does not tread on the toes of his constituents, unless it is very necessary.

Indira was of the opinion that it was an important part of her life's mission to help her father in his task as Prime Minister. She felt that under the circumstances, since he was a widower and very much alone, he needed all the assistance she could give. She was an enthusiastic supporter of his efforts, which she considered to be in the right direction, and a frank critic of those programs which she considered to be in error. Knowing Indira's dedication to the welfare of the people, her broad understanding and unselfishness, Nehru respected her views. It should also be remembered that, whereas many Indian leaders might have been hesitant to criticize Nehru in his august presence, Indira was unafraid.

In 1948, Indira accompanied her father to the Commonwealth Prime Ministers' Conference held in London. This was a unique opportunity for her to come in contact with the leaders of the various nations and to view the problems of India from the perspective of the Commonwealth group of nations. Although one section of Indian public opinion had strongly resented Commonwealth ties, Indira, like her father, recognized that India would have many advantages, politically and economically, by being a member of a group of nations with cultural and political ties. One of the reasons that had persuaded Indian leaders to remain in the Commonwealth was the prospect of having "reliable friends" in the event of aggression.

After the Commonwealth Prime Ministers' Conference, Nehru addressed the United Nations General Assembly in Paris on November 3, 1948. This was a world stage for the great Asian leader. Indira would long remember with pride the masterly address given by her father. The powerful voice of Asia would henceforth be heard in the councils of nations.

One of the milestones in the distinguished career of Nehru was the organization of the Asian Relations Conference, which attempted to unite the people of Asia for freedom, peace and prosperity. This conference grew in size and eventually included African nations also. In January, 1949, the Asian Relations Conference, representing nineteen nations, was held in New Delhi to protest against Dutch Police action. Nehru was the chief leader, and once again Indira had the splendid opportunity of conversing with other Asian leaders and getting a first-hand impression of their national problems.

In 1949, Nehru paid an official visit to the United States. He took Indira along to serve as his hostess and companion. The reception throughout America was grand. The government and public alike "rolled out the red carpet." There was a full blast of publicity with all its fanfare. It was a hero's welcome inclusive of the ticker tape parade on New York's Fifth Avenue. Indira enjoyed the friendship and warmth of the people. She was greatly impressed by America's advance in providing the "good life" for its people. Concerning what she saw of America's bounty, she wrote that the abundance of luxury would have to be seen to be believed. Even the animals in America had it good. (A journalist said, and truthfully so, that the dogs in America are better fed than millions of human beings around the world.)

In 1955, Nehru took Indira along during his tours in the Soviet Union, Poland and Yugoslavia. Received everywhere with warmth and cordiality, she responded with enthusiasm in meeting people and visiting centers of special interest. It so happened that several newborn Russian babies were named Indira in honor of the distinguished guest.

In spite of frailty in appearance and the overwhelming demands of travels and meetings, Indira kept pace with her stalwart father in his journeys at home and abroad. The general elections of 1952 required Herculean effort on her father's part. Indira went with him everywhere. They had to use all modes of transportation—plane, train, car, even bullock cart. There was also a lot of walking to do. Life was "rough and tumble" in the intense heat, among restless crowds along the way and at the meetings. The "one-man" job done by Nehru is best described by his biographer, Michael Brecher, who said: "The Congress (election) campaign was a one-man affair—Nehru, Nehru and more Nehru. He was chief of staff, field commander—spokesman and foot-soldier at one and the same time." In and through all the strain and struggle, Indira was a steady source of comfort, help and guidance for the weary Prime Minister. In many respects, she was an indispensable help to her aging father.

During this time she was under constant pressure to take an active part in politics and to contest an election to Parliament. This she refused as she considered that looking after her father was for the time being the best service she could render to the nation.

However, she was elected to the twenty-one member working committee and secured the highest number of votes. This committee had authority in approving candidates for state Legislatures and Parliaments and in finalizing the party's platform. As usual, Indira went all out to do her work. She met with all kinds of people and addressed numerous meetings. Everywhere she was a great attraction. Along with her work as a member of the Congress Election Committee and the Congress Disciplinary Action Committee, she gave much needed leadership by organizing the Village Contact Movement. This was an effort at "grass roots" involvement of the national party with the problems of the villagers, who constituted nearly seventy-five percent of India's population.

Besides the party work, she also used every available opportunity to encourage those in official positions to get things done for public causes. She participated directly in many charities and social welfare projects.

In April, 1955, twenty-nine Asian-African nations met in a conference in Bandung, Indonesia, under the sponsorship of Nehru, U Nu of Burma and other eminent Asian-African leaders. The conference rejected all forms of colonialism. It was not a conference against anyone (as some quarters chose to think), but for freedom and justice. Having suffered so much and so long the staggering adversities of colonial conditions, Nehru and other leaders were determined that Asian-African nations should work to end colonialism in all its forms.

Indira had the good fortune of attending this conference along with her father. It is said that she diligently attended all deliberations and met all the delegations. Several of the leaders there expressed their admiration for her grasp of international affairs and competence in suggesting solutions to complex problems.

On June 21, Indira accompanied her father to the Commonwealth Prime Ministers' Conference in London and later made visits to Ireland, West Germany, Yugoslavia, France and Greece.

In the following year she made many other international tours in the company of her father, including visits to Egypt, the Soviet Union, Czechoslovakia, Poland and Austria. It may be noted here that in spite of the natural temptations of sight-seeing, Indira concentrated upon the work of her father in his efforts to find ways and means of ending the Cold War and of establishing durable foundations for international peace and security.

As a result of the many journeys with her father and other public duties she was away from her husband frequently. It caused considerable strain in their relationship. No doubt, Indira and Feroze had from the beginning certain difficulties in adjusting to each other. Also, any man who marries a woman who is a celebrity is in for lots of strain and stress, and in this case the woman happened to be the famous daughter of Prime Minister Nehru.

Their romance had begun very naturally and in

time had blossomed and fructified into marriage. They were happy together in family life and in the adventures of the freedom struggle. Then two things happened which upset their tranquility. First, Nehru became Prime Minister of India in 1947. Secondly, he invited Indira and Feroze to live with him. Feroze, the freedom fighter and husband, was henceforth the Prime Minister's son-in-law. He had to put up with some of the formalities and officiousness of the Prime Minister's residence. These were adverse to his nature.

Indira and Feroze were deeply in love. But they were also both young, inexperienced and headstrong. Both had independent ways. However, since they were devoted to Nehru, it would have been possible by means of wise counseling to prevent much of the strain and stress they passed through in their relationship. Evidently, they were not fortunate enough to have had the necessary counseling.

Many have wondered how Indira could reconcile the absorption in the care for her father with her duties as a wife. Did her husband feel neglected? Or did he see eye to eye with his wife in the prime need of looking after the Prime Minister?

Feroze was a young man dedicated to a political career. He was elected to Parliament and soon moved to official quarters. Thus, Feroze's career and Nehru's need for the care of his daughter brought a breech in their living together. Feroze, of course, was busy with his many duties as a Member of Parliament from the Rae Bareli constituency and Indira, in turn, was busy as hostess to the Prime Minister. However, they got together

whenever possible. Their two sons were in boarding
school, but during the holidays they came to Delhi.
As a practice, Feroze and Indira would receive them
together. The family set-up was not ideal, and
though it may be difficult for Americans to understand, the couple could put up with it as they were
used to the ideals of renunciation so characteristic
of India's freedom struggle. From childhood Indira
had learned to forsake personal pleasures, comforts
and advantages for the freedom of the nation. Now
in her thought, it was clear that the best way she
could help further the interest of the nation was
by helping her father, the leader of the nation.
Feroze probably could see this matter in the perspective of his own experience in India's freedom
struggle and his dedication to the advancement of
the people. To the Nehru family, freedom and the
good of the country were above personal as well as
family security and welfare. Feroze, himself an
ardent idealist and worker for India's freedom, made
some accommodation in his mind, however difficult,
to permit his "helpmate" to help the aging leader
of India's continuing freedom struggle (for itself
and for all mankind).

Indira Gandhi has been always mindful of what
is taught in the Upanishads. "Thou shalt not be
negligent of social welfare." She has spent more
time in social work than politics and has been the
leader of several organizations dedicated to social
service. Besides working with organizations, she
took a personal interest in the welfare of the destitute and the handicapped.

A most touching example of her compassion for

the handicapped is the case of Satya Danphhi, daughter of a railway worker who was murdered during the communal riots in Delhi. Satya was twenty years old, but unable to walk because of a childhood accident in which she was run over by a train and lost both legs. Thus, she had to drag herself around. Indira searched far and wide to see if she could be provided with artificial legs. She came to know that there was only one institution in India which manufactured artificial limbs, the Artificial Limb Center at Poona, and that it was limited to the use of the military. Hence Indira found it very difficult to proceed further. However, she finally succeeded in persuading the Defense Minister, Baldev Singh, to make an exception. It was done and, as a result, the service of the center was thrown open to civilians also.

It took several months for Satya to be treated and fitted with the artificial legs. The long waiting often gave her fits of depression. Sometimes it seemed as though she was about to give up. Then she would go to Indira for guidance and inspiration. Finally, she was fitted with the legs and acquired the facility to use them as though they were natural. Satya was physicially and psychologically uplifted. Beaming with joy she came to Indira to display her newly won facilities and to announce her engagement. Needless to say, that was a thrilling moment of satisfaction for Indira, who had labored a long time for it. She wrote that Satya was "positively scattering the gold dust of her happiness on all who happened to be near. Every now and then when I seem to be going around in circles, when my efforts

seem so feeble compared with the immensity of the
task, the memory of Satya's radiance, like Wordsworth and his 'Daffodils', comes to mind and I cannot help myself smiling.

"In those days of 1929-31, I am talking about,"
says Indira with deep feeling, "when there was
firing, even though people were severely injured,
no doctor could come to treat them. The doctor
could only come when it was dark—when nobody
could see that he was coming and report him to
the government. So, once when such firing took
place in a village not far from our home, we had
to go ourselves to help these wounded and bleeding
young boys, most of them between the ages of fourteen and seventeen. We opened part of our own
home as a hospital ward. This was my introduction
to service because I was only twelve or thirteen at
the time. But, since we could not get anyone else,
my friends and I had to be nurses for those very
seriously wounded people."

Indira's association with service agencies and
active field work began at about the age of ten,
when every Sunday she bicycled out to Naini, six
miles out of Allahabad, to work in a Home for
Lepers. At the age of twelve she organized a
children's section of Gandhi's Charkha Sangh devoted to handspinning. Also, she took the lead in
establishing the Allahabad branch of the children's
brigade, known popularly as *Vanara Sena* or the
Monkey Brigade. It was a volunteer group of teen-
agers who aided the Congress by carrying messages,
singing and hanging national flags, cooking food
and giving first aid to Congress volunteers hurt in

police lathi charges. At one time, the Monkey Brigade had as many as 6,000 members.

There is an interesting story connected with Indira's founding of a Children's Cooperative in Delhi, known today as *The Balsahayog*. One day when she was shopping in Connaught Place, New Delhi, a ragged little boy approached her and tried to sell combs. She did not purchase one. But the persistent boy trailed Indira from store to store. Finally, she felt constrained to buy a comb. Of this encounter Indira said: "He was a beautiful child. We talked and I asked when he went to school. He worked all day. He didn't go to school and made two rupees a day."

As a result of this experience, Indira took the initiative to establish *The Balsahayog*. Here in a one story building within a spacious compound, boys worked at different trades—carpentry, tailoring, woodwork and canework. Some worked in the garden and grew vegetables.

Indira has served as the President of the Indian Council for Child Welfare. A member of the board of trustees of the Kamala Nehru Memorial Hospital and chairman of the *Gram Bharati*, a rural institute at Allahabad, she has exercised much influence in coordinating the efforts of various government and voluntary organizations so that welfare programs can be administered more adequately and efficiently. Special emphasis has also been laid on preventive aspects of the programs. She has been the recipient of many honors in recognition of her services and achievements. Among them mention may be made especially of the Mother's Award of the United

States (1953), the Howland Memorial Prize of Yale University and the Italian Isbella D'Este for outstanding service in the field of international relations.

Like her illustrious father and grandfather, Indira is a person of varied interests and of a deep compassion that extends even to the animals. Within the walls of her grounds as well as within the residence, she has had a menagerie of all sorts of pets. The house was alive with parrots, pigeons, squirrels, dogs and other pets. She also had a special interest in bird watching. Besides being hostess to the Prime Minister and having other official duties, she had her hands full taking care of her menagerie. On a visit to Assam, she and her children were presented with a baby cat bear (a red Panda). Indira and the boys studied the books on Indian animals carefully and identified the species to which the Panda belonged. The tribesman who presented the animal had called it a bear. Hoping that one day this tiny ball of fur would grow into a great big bear, they called it Bhima (after the giant Bhima of the Epic Mahabharata).

Chapter VI

CONGRESS PRESIDENT

In the year 1946, when discussions were going on between the British Cabinet Mission and Indian leaders, the writer had a very interesting visit with Mahatma Gandhi. Among other things, the writer told him of the concern expressed by a saintly Christion leader, Mr. K.C. Chacko (one of the founders of the Union Christian College in Kerala), about the food problem and some constructive suggestions for its solution. One of the suggestions was that Gandhi should, in the interests of the people, serve as Food Minister. Gandhi smiled a great big smile, and made it very clear that he had no thoughts of a job for himself. The great leader never asked for jobs, but jobs went begging after him. So it was in the case of Nehru, and so it is in the case of his "beloved to the sight," Indira Priyadarshini.

In 1959, when U.N. Dhebar, President of the Indian National Congress Party, resigned in the middle of his term, Indira was approached by party leaders to get her consent for election to the presidency. She expressed reluctance. Pressure was exerted from important quarters, including former President Dhebar. While she was touring her father's constituency in Allahabad district, she received a message to the effect that she was unanimously elected Congress President. She accepted. However she resigned after half of her two-year term. The reason, as she stated, was that her first duty was to look after her father who had passed seventy and had begun to feel the debilitating effects of age and exhaustion.

It is interesting to note that Indira was the third person in the Nehru family to be elected President of the Congress Party. First it was her grandfather, Motilal (1919 and 1928), and then her father, who was elected and re-elected six times.

The election of Indira was a recognition of her own political personality. Nehru always took elaborate pains never to use his influence to push his daughter forward into a position of power. At the same time he had a proud father's confidence in her capacity to rise to the occasion if and when she would be called upon in her own right: "I remained neutral, and I am told even by people who do not like me or my policies that she made a very good President. Sometimes she chose a line of her own against my way of thinking, which was the right thing to do. . .Indira has a strong independent mind of her own, as she should have. That is all. . .I am neither preparing her for anything, nor do I propose to prevent her from taking any responsibilities the country or the people may desire of her." Only a few months before his death, Nehru mentioned a "collective leadership" (of Kamaraj, Shastri and Nanda) as a possible successor government and denied explicitly that he was grooming anyone. He added: "That does not mean she should not be called to occupy any position of responsibility after me." The far-sighted father could not but have had some vision of the far-reaching possibilities of his daughter's services.

Indira took office when she was only forty-two. Congress prestige had hit a new low. Over the years the office of Congress President had declined in authority and prestige. While the Congress was engaged in the freedom struggle, the people were united against a common foe, namely an imperial power. They were inspired by the prospect of freedom. They were uplifted by the vibrant leadership of Mahatma Gandhi, Jawaharlal Nehru, Vallabbhai Patel, Rajendra Prasad and others. The sacrifices of the leaders for the cause of liberty had stirred the masses to make sacrifices and to suffer poverty and allied miseries without grumbling. The leaders had made promises of a happy future to come in an independent India. The people believed. However, after the achievement of political power, the masses went through a period of disillusionment. They found that even after years in office, the Congress Party had not succeeded in adequately solving the many problems of India's poverty, food shortage, unemployment, slum conditions, inflation and black market. The opposition parties degraded the Congress leadership because of nepotism, self-seeking and bureaucratic maze. They also accused them of the arrogance of power, luxurious living and corruption.

There were also other reasons for the decline in the stature of the Congress Party. With the Parliamentary set-up of the Administration, the center of power naturally moved from the Congress

Party to the Parliament. For some time Prime
Minister Nehru continued to be President of the
Congress. This in some ways blurred the identity
of the Congress Party leadership. Further, such
a set-up naturally made the Congress the recep-
tacle of criticism for all the many faults of the administration. Later, the Congress was headed by
other leaders who were not able to cope adequately
with the massive problems they had inherited. The
organization was threatening to split. There was
neither unity of purpose, nor unity of action. At
the election of 1957, Congress had lost one state,
Kerala, to the Communists, and at the next election, 1962, it was expected to lose a few more. Indira had not sought the office of Congress President,
the office sought her. She was reluctant to accept it,
but was constrained to do so by persuasion from
Congress leaders.

Indira's election to the Congress Presidency was
a great inspiration to youth and women. During her
tenure of one year, capable young workers were
promoted. Inefficient party officials were quietly
dropped. Women took a larger part in the Congress
proceedings. Cooperation of non-party members was
sought. She emphasized positive and constructive
efforts. Her programs and contacts with the people
seemed to bring a new sense of unity to the land.

Like her illustrious father, she emphasized the
need for the eradication of fear and superstition.
She encouraged the development of research and
scientific planning. No time was spent in advocating any political theory. Her concern was to adopt
methods that would hasten the development of the

country and provide solutions to the problems of poverty, unemployment and illiteracy. However, she was not in favor of the rapid fire methods of communism, leading to regimentation and restriction of individual liberty. She was confident that out of the moral heritage and culture of India, the people could, with the use of the scientific method, develop their own way of advancing the interests of the country. Indira stated that "in India we have something as special as any other country with its own legends. We would not like to lose that personality and the toleration of different views, especially the diversity in our unity. On the other hand, we just cannot concentrate on fighting communism. We have to succeed in a positive program of providing basic amenities and raising our low living standards. But I do not believe in the sort of individual freedom that restricts other people's freedom."

As Congress President, she encouraged women to work sincerely and efficiently in social welfare and political fields. She advised them to leave behind age-old traditions and superstitions which held them back; she exhorted them to keep in step with the progress of the times and to develop a wider outlook in national and world affairs.

Indira cautioned women to give priority to their home and children. She felt that women, while maintaining their womanliness, could make an important contribution to public life.

At her first press conference as Congress President, Indira said, "The nation is in a hurry and we can't afford to lose time. My complaint against Congress is that it isn't going as fast as the people are advancing."

The new President entered office with considerable devotion and experience. However, since she served for only one year, she was able to do only a few of the many things she was concerned with. She had been a political and social welfare worker all her life. She had very direct experience in the functioning of the Congress hierarchy as she had served as a member of the Congress Working Committee. Although she was never known for personal ambitions of a political nature, she was always noted for enthusiasm to do well whatever job was entrusted to her. Indira tried to overhaul the Congress leadership; to this end, she substituted younger people in her Working Committee. And, perhaps as a gesture of her independence, she added the name of her father to the older people who were dropped from the Working Committee. He had been a member of this Committee for thirty-seven years and it took courage to drop him from this all-powerful group. (Of course, as Prime Minister, he was invited to the meetings.) Indira was very businesslike in the conduct of meetings. She got a great deal of work done by exercising diplomatic control over both leaders (including her father) and followers who were used to long-winded talks.

When she took office as Congress President, Congress ministries were in office in all states except Kerala. There, in a multiple party contest, the communists emerged as the party with the largest number of seats in the legislature. They had less than fifty percent of the seats and were able to form a ministry only with the help of leftist-inclined independents. To many Congressmen this meant a loss of face. Their party's monopoly of power had been broken. They did not realize that the coming to power of a communist ministry in Kerala would have world-wide implications. This event was heralded as a first instance of the communists forming the Ministry of a state through the "ballot box." The people of Kerala, by voting for the communists, had voted against the failure of the Congress ministries to solve their problems. The state moved in the spotlight nationally and internationally.

It was an unprecedented situation in which the communists came into power by the use of the ballot box. Its success or failure could have world-wide implications for the future of communist parties. Some ventured to say that this was a forerunner for the establishment of communism through parliamentary democracy on a national basis.

For a time the communist government seemed secure because of the constitutional and electoral justification it enjoyed. The masses were hopeful that the new ministry would cut through the red tape maze of Congress ministries, bring about social and economic reforms, and cope with the mounting problems of rising prices, unemployment and food shortage.

The communist ministry was headed by a skilled diplomat and intellectual, Mr. E.M.S. Namboodripad. Though born in the highest caste, he had relinquished his privileges and comforts to identify himself with the masses. His competence as a speaker and writer won him mass appeal. For years he had to function "underground," as communists had been barred in Kerala. Yet, he enjoyed enormous popularity. Although an indefatigable organizer and speaker, he did not have any administrative experience as far as government was concerned.

After having been in power for a while, the communist ministry was charged by the opposition with creating conditions to insure the perpetuation of their administration. Troubles reached a peak when the communist government introduced a bill for educational reform which appeared to various religious groups, such as the Roman Catholics, as a form of state regimentation and interference with religious freedom. The Nair Service Society headed by Mr. Mannath Padmanabha Pillai joined with the Catholics in their resistance to the interference of government in educational and social concerns. The Congress Party, which was very anxious to throw out the communists, joined with the Praja Socialists, Roman Catholics and Nair Service Society in their determined efforts to end this regime.

Indira, who was well apprised of the developments, drew the attention of other national leaders to Kerala. She made it clear that the Congress, as the opposition party in Kerala, had every right to agitate for the removal of the ministry. It was understood that all the programs used for this purpose would be of a peaceful nature. Under the leadership of Mr. Mannath Padmanabha Pillai, a statewide agitation of unprecedented momentum started. There were strikes, walkouts from schools, demonstrations, mass meetings and fasts. Government machinery, including transportation and communication, was seriously blocked.

The desperate efforts of the Ministry to end the

struggle failed. Indira held the view that the ministry, through its disregard of the Constitution, forfeited its right to continue in office. So she recommended that the central government take immediate action to provide an opportunity for the people for fresh elections and a new mandate.

As the constitutional head, the President of India, Dr. Rajendra Prasad, stepped in. He dismissed the ministry and established President's rule in order to pave the way for a new general election. The chief justification given for such a step was that public agitation against the ministry had become so massive that the state government was unable to prevent the danger of violence and lawlessness.

The central government ordered that general elections be held after six months. Indira, as Congress President, had to give leadership to ensure that the communists did not secure a second victory at the polls after they had been ousted. In the Kerala situation, she showed aggressive leadership. In her election strategy she approached politics with a pragmatic and realistic perspective. She permitted the Congress to enter into electoral alliances with the Praja Socialist Party. This alliance was generally approved by the public, as the Praja Socialist Party was dedicated to democratic socialism; this the Congress also had accepted. It also had the advantage of dynamic and well-experienced leadership in the person of Mr. Pattom Thanu Pillai. In further strengthening the non-communist front, an electoral alliance was entered into with the Muslim League (noted for its communal platform). This move was criticized by many in the country because they

remembered that in 1947, the All-India Muslim League was responsible for the partition of India into
Pakistan and India, with the claim that Muslims
being a majority in two areas of India they should
be made into a separate state of Pakistan. However,
it may be stated here that the Muslim League of
Kerala had settled down in its program as a provincial party concerned with the promotion of the
interests of Muslims. This was not anything strange
in a state where there are various organizations like
the Christian Congress of the Christians, Nair Service Society of Nairs (a section of Hindus) and Sad-
hu Narayana Dharma Paripalana Sangham (a Service Society for a somewhat deprived section of the
Hindus). As far as Kerala was concerned, electoral
alliances with a communal group like the Muslim
League were not shocking, although in many quarters in North India (which has painful memories of
the days of violence connected with India's partition) such a step was highly disconcerting.

The United Front led by the Congress had a resounding victory at the polls, and a coalition ministry was formed in Kerala headed by the Praja
Socialist Party (P.S.P.) leader Pattom Thanu Pillai. The results of the election showed a decrease
from sixty to twenty-nine seats in the communist
strength. However, they did poll forty-three percent of the votes, whereas it was only slightly more
than thirty-five percent in the 1957 election. The anti-
communist United Front was able to secure ninety-
three seats and hence an overwhelming majority.

During one of her tours of duty as Congress President Indira received the news that Feroze had been

stricken with a heart attack. It came as a total shock to her. Leaving everything aside she hastened to his side. Since Feroze had been in the best of health, Indira had no hint that anything was wrong with her husband's robust constitution.

Indira, with much loving care, nursed him back to health. When he was well enough to travel, the entire family took a long delayed vacation trip. It was like a second honeymoon. The affection of his family, and the cool, invigorating climate of Kashmir made Feroze recover splendidly.

Returning home, they resumed their political responsibilities. It was on September 8, 1960 that Feroze suffered his final and fatal heart attack. Indira, overcome with grief, went into a period of mourning. The young widow was only forty-two. She wept bitterly. Writing to a friend, she said she felt "lost. . .desolate and dead inside."

Feroze had been a young man with a promising future in politics. He was a loyal and dedicated party worker. Many prominent people gave glowing tributes to his name. He was missed not only by his family, but by all of India. The sentiments of his fellow parliamentarians were best expressed in the tribute by Asoka Mehta, the then chairman of the Praja Socialist Party and later a Minister of the Central Government. "Death robs Parliament of an outstanding member and the underprivileged of a tireless champion. His sympathies were as catholic as his interests were wide. . . ."

For a time nothing seemed to console Indira. Through work, she tried to keep her mind off her bereavement. She found solace in looking after her

aging father and in taking care of the seemingly endless tasks awaiting her in the national and international fields. Soon Indira was appointed a member
of the Indian delegation to UNESCO in Paris. She
served in this capacity with distinction from 1960-
64. Later she was elected a member of the Executive Board of UNESCO.

Perhaps the most serious shock experienced by
Indira during her tenure as her father's companion
was the Chinese invasion of India. It had so cruelly
shattered Nehru's confidence in peaceful co-existence and his hopes for peace in Asia, that observers
noted that within the year he had visibly aged at
least ten years. A lot of his natural ebullience was
gone for good. Some friends went to the extent of
saying that the Chinese aggression had so deeply
hurt the ideals cherished by Nehru that his inner
suffering had cut down many years from his life.

His shrewd daughter did not suffer so much disillusionment and frustration because she had foreseen
such a consequence and had warned her father. She
had visited China in 1954. With great concern she
had observed the vast military preparations of
China and had conveyed her alarm to Nehru. But
her father was in no mood to accept any alarming
view in an atmosphere resounding with the slogan
"Hindi-Chini Bhai Bhai" ("Indians and Chinese
are brothers).

The great Nehru, like Neville Chamberlain, had
the English training which accepts the words of the
opponent as honest. Even as Chamberlain believed
in the Munich Pact, Nehru trusted the agreement
by the Chinese Premier Chou-En-Lai to abide by

Panchshila (the five principles of foreign policy):
mutual respect for each other's territorial integrity;
mutual non-aggression; mutual non-interference in
each other's internal affairs; equality and mutual
benefit; and peaceful co-existence. In the case of
Chamberlain and Nehru it was a case of honest men
taking for granted the integrity of national leaders
with whom they dealt. And in both cases the trust
was misplaced. "And what a fall my countrymen!"

During the Chinese attack on India, Indira worked
tirelessly and arranged various services for the welfare of the soldiers. Even against the wishes of her
father and friends like Lal Bahadur Shastri, she
visited the front lines and helped boost the morale
of the fighting man. As chairman of the Citizens Central Council, formed in 1962 to mobilize the country's war efforts, she gave outstanding leadership.
It is said that she did a marvellous job in building
up the morale of the masses as well as the soldiers.
She visited the front, organized rallies, spoke at
numerous meetings and raised funds for national defense. Indeed, she helped her father to rally the nation in the hour of its trial and tribulation.

Chapter VII

NEHRU AND AFTER

Towards the end of Nehru's lifetime, the question was continually being asked, "After Nehru what?" However, neither Nehru nor anyone else attempted to answer it. Naturally, there were alarmists in some countries who concluded that after Nehru would come "chaos." Most people could not think of anyone who could do his job.

Over a forty-year period, including eighteen as Prime Minister, Nehru had established himself in a most formidable position. As an administrator, he appeared irreplaceable and as a figurehead he seemed indispensable. Yet, much of the blame for not grooming young men for future leadership must fall to Nehru, who did not hand-pick any bright young men to follow in his footsteps. At the same time, however, the training of younger leaders is going on all the time in India. The Congress Party has, without much publicity or fanfare, been training young men in every section of India.

Of course, as a politician, Nehru had not specified who might replace him. Yet, from his actions in the last years of his life, it can be said that he thought Lal Bahadur Shastri to be the most capable person to continue the work he had started. This did not show favoritism; India already knew the qualities

126

of mind and heart that made Shastri the obvious choice to take control when Nehru passed on.

Shastri had played an important role in India's freedom struggle. His integrity and incorruptibility were well-known and he had worked closely with Nehru for over thirty years. During the latter part of this period, Nehru had given him more and more responsibility and each time it was a job "well done."

In January, 1964, after Nehru suffered a stroke, it was clear to top party officials that he might not live for long. As a precaution, to insure that his policies would be continued, they began making some moves. One such move was a letter by twelve chief ministers of the states to include Indira in the existing cabinet. This effort never got off the ground, as Indira refused it.

From January to May, Indira concentrated on nursing her father and helping him regain his health. She was always on hand to limit the number of visitors, to answer the mail, to make him obey the doctors' orders and, in general, to brief him about all current developments. Slowly, Nehru's health improved. In May, he was strong enough to attend a session of the All-India Congress Committee in Bombay.

During his convalescence, Nehru still functioned as Prime Minister, although it is well-known that Indira helped him perform his governing tasks. In fact, she undoubtedly made many decisions on his behalf.

After a brief holiday at Dehra Dun, father and daughter returned to New Delhi on May 26. Spectators at the airport were visibly impressed with Nehru's improved health. That night, as was his usual custom, Nehru cleared his desk. Surveying what he had accomplished, he said, "I think we have finished everything." Then he retired for the night.

The next morning he suffered a stroke, collapsed and never again regained consciousness. His grief-stricken daughter noted that there was a Robert Frost poem scribbled on her father's writing pad. They were his favorite lines:

> The woods are lovely, dark and deep
> But I have promises to keep
> And miles to go before I sleep. . . .

Indira was heartbroken. She had seen the deaths of so many loved ones — her grandfather, her mother, her husband and now her father. Suddenly, life seemed dark and desolate for her. That night she kept the all-night vigil. She grieved, but, as her father had taught her, controlled her emotions. For twenty-four hours she did not touch any food; she did not want to eat. Yet, with her sense of duty and concern for others, she had the cooks prepare food for all those in the house. After they had been fed, she told them to take baths and return properly dressed for the funeral. "You know," she told them, "that Papu would never like you in this dishevelled state to accompany him on his last journey."

Submerging her personal sorrow, she was equal to her responsibilities, taking great pains to see that all the many details for the funeral were arranged. The next day saw an overwhelming expression of the sorrow and tribute of India's masses for their

beloved hero. As the funeral procession wended its
way over a six-mile route to the river bank, thousands lined the streets to shower flowers and to
have a last look at the "precious jewel" of India.
The nation and the world mourned him. His work
was done and he was gone from this earth. And
to Indira Priyadarshini ("beloved to the sight" as
her Papu named her), the loss of her Papu, the
friend, philosopher, guide and inspirer, left a bitter
and grievous void which could never be filled. In the
privacy of her room she wept.

Nehru had made it quite clear that he did not
want religious rites connected with his funeral. However, Indira made a personal and independent decision to have the traditional religious rites for cremation. Although it might appear to be contrary to the
ideas of her father, she found necessary justification for the step. Love is said to cover a multitude
of sins. In this instance, her love for her father
prompted her to do it. Indira is a lady with deep
faith and understanding of religious philosophy.
Out of her own religious experience and compre-
hension of the eternal nature of life and the spiritual
source thereof, she could not possibly dismiss the
cremation of the body as the end of all. She would
not want to neglect the opportunity of recognizing
the inspiring thoughts embodied in India's religious
and cultural heritage. In life and in death she wanted
her Papu to have the best service. After all, her
father was only an agnostic, not a nihilist. And if
you judge a person by his actions, who could be more
religious than Nehru, the servant of his people, who
stood for the highest principles of life and sacrificed

so much for the good of his country? What is more religious than truth, justice and compassion? Who in India had more of those qualities in life than Nehru?

This was a terminus for Indira, in a physical sense, of a life-long association of the warmest and most affectionate nature. No doubt it was the most fruitful and rewarding association of her life. Indeed, this might well be history's most helpful and significant association between a father and a daughter. Where else has a father and daughter joined together for a freedom struggle which called for the sacrifice of everything, even the most precious thing in life, life itself? Where else has a daughter been elected Prime Minister to follow the footsteps of her father in the leadership of five hundred million people?

It is stated that at the time of the death of Nehru, the attitude of many Congress leaders was such that Indira would have been chosen Prime Minister if she had shown interest for the job. Lal Bahadur Shastri, himself, was so loyal and devoted to the Nehru family that he would have supported any move to this end. It is said that when Indira made it clear she was not "running" for anything, the obvious choice was Shastri. For her, the previous few years had been marked by hard work, some triumphs and some tragedies. The two most important persons in her life, first her husband, then her father, were gone from this earth. Her two sons, Rajiv and Sanjaya, had to be sent to boarding school. Indira was alone to find her new bearings and to contemplate the future of her life's dedication. But she could not contemplate too long.

During his illness, Nehru gave Lal Bahadur a chance to do all the work that he, himself, had been doing. The latter made good in every way. And how he made good is a question that no superficial observer can answer. It is here that we confront the inner strength, certitude and selfless devotion of Nehru's protege. It is here that we recognize the power of the will, "that force unseen" which "can hew away to any goal, though walls of granite intervene."

Shastri was chosen unanimously to be the successor. Recognizing the wide experience and contact that Indira had in world affairs in the company of her father (who held the portfolios of Prime Minister and Foreign Minister), Shastri offered her the portfolio of Foreign Minister. However, she graciously turned it down. The next offer was that of Minister for Information and Broadcasting. She accepted. Thus, Indira was placed in the fourth rank in the ministry. Later she was elected unopposed to Rajya Sabha (upper House of Parliament). In spite of all the stress and strain of family and national life, Indira had consistently taken interest in the arts. She recognized that the primary needs of the people are food, clothing and shelter, but at the same time she said that everything should be done to develop the cultural life also. It might be remembered here that both in Poona and in Shantiniketan, she had participated in music, dance and the other arts. She had a great love for folk dances and especially for the Manipuri, which she was able to dance very beautifully. During her stay in England, she often attended plays and operas.

Because of the importance of the movies in India, she had worked with the Film Society, first as its President and then as its Vice-President. Indira had the clear view that the movies provided one of the best media of entertainment and education for the people. Hence, she was anxious to help its development in the best of lines, free from bureaucratic red tape and prudish censorship.

Naturally, the Information Ministry turned out to be an excellent place for the exercise of the talents of this lover of the arts. Many achievements are credited to her during her one year of stewardship. Like her father, she started the practice of clearing the desk each day. Official business was handled with dispatch.

The great possibilities of the television media for education and entertainment encouraged her to give top priority to the project of starting regular TV programs in India. The social worker latent in her found a most remarkable expression when she authorized the New Delhi TV station to televise for village women an educational program on the use of contraceptives in family planning.

She did not succumb to political prejudices or pressures. Neither did she allow patronage or political considerations to affect the minister's decision. The officials who often hesitated to make decisions for fear of "political reprisals" felt that a new era of responsible initiative had arrived with the new Information Minister.

Indira was the first Indian Minister invited to Moscow after the replacement of Khrushchev by Kosygin. Her visit to Moscow convinced her that the Soviet attitude toward India and China would not be changed. She also received assurances from the Soviet government concerning continuation of Soviet economic aid to India.

Several weeks later she was in New York to inaugurate the Nehru Memorial Exhibition. Like her father, she strived to maintain good relations with both the United States and the Soviet Union.

In January, 1965, the Government of India held the International Film Festival of India. Indira took deep interest in the festival, and especially in the films that were received and exhibited, as well as the entertainment of the members of the jury and other participants.

Indira started the practice of "person-to-person" broadcasts, which had a large outreach among the masses as a means of instruction and contacts. She was also interested in giving a new look to the All India Radio which, she felt, should function as an independent cultural agency. In addition, she visualized the 100-crore Master Plan for the development of radio and television.

Besides her ministerial responsibilities, Indira took an active interest in political and social activities. She wrote on "Social Service" in which she gave the essence of her experience as a social worker.

Perhaps, the most important event that took place during Indira's stewardship of the Information Ministry, was the war between India and Pakistan. As usual, Indira went all out to help in the war effort. She went to the front and encouraged the soldiers by her visits. She was the first Indian leader to reach Kashmir when armed infiltrators threatened the state. She is well remembered for the slogan she popularized: "We are Indians; let none divide us." In securing contributions for the National Defense Fund, she rendered outstanding service. The legacy of conflict as well as the triumph and tragedy that followed at the Tashkent Peace Conference had a tremendous impact on Indira's life and future work.

A democratic country, while mourning the loss of a departed leader, has to maintain serenity to choose a new standard bearer so that "the government of the people" shall continue and prosper. Just as the United States, in the hour of the tragic death of John F. Kennedy, turned to Lyndon Baines Johnson, India in its agony at the sudden demise of Lal Bahadur Shastri turned to Indira Priyadarshini Gandhi to carry the torch.

Chapter VIII

MADAME PRIME MINISTER

January 19, 1966 was a red letter day in India's history and in Indira's life. It was the day for which she had been groomed through years of training, apprenticeship, discipline and suffering. As her second name Priyadarshini indicates, she was "dear to the sight" to the people who loved her and put so much confidence in her. As the day dawned, even while the mist hovered over Delhi, Indira, true to her commitment, took the pilgrimage first to Rajaghat (the place hallowed to the memory of Mahatma Gandhi) and then to the nearby Shantivana, (the memorial garden dedicated to her father). Later, she drove to Teen Murti House where she had lived with her father. There she stood with folded arms and bowed head in front of the favorite portrait of her father and rededicated herself as a servant of her country's progress. Experiencing a vistavision of treasured memories, affection and gratitude welled up within her.

After thus honoring the memory of her father and the father of the nation, Indira, with fervent steps and lofty emotions, arrived at the Parliament Hall. The daughter of Nehru brought to the Parliament many grateful memories and patriotic

135

feelings. The Parliamentarians, in turn, gave her a standing ovation. She moved about calmly, collectedly and cheerfully, greeting friends and acquaintances. She even took the initiative to go and greet her opponent, Mr. Morarji Desai (who was the only other candidate for the Prime Minister's Office), to seek his blessings. It was not long before the election concluded and Indira won the day in a setting of high drama.

Rising above intraparty struggles, she declared, "I thank those who voted for me and those who voted against me.... Once elections are over it is only fit and proper that differences should be forgotten and we should all work together." Thus, she underscored the validity and propriety of the democratic process.

After the election, in a talk with a friend, Indira referred to Robert Frost's poem "How Hard It Is to Keep from Being King When It's in You and in the Situation."

> *The King said to his son: "Enough of this!*
> *The Kingdom's yours to finish as you please.*
> *I'm getting out tonight. Here, take the crown."*
> *But the Prince drew away his hand in time*
> *To avoid what he wasn't sure he wanted.*

Was Indira sure she wanted the crown—" a crown of thorns?" The answer is in her actions. She was sworn in as Prime Minister on January 24. In her first broadcast to the nation on Republic Day (January 26, 1966), she pledged herself anew to the ideals of the builders of the nation, to democracy and secularism, to planned economic and social advancement, to peace and friendship among nations. "Peace we want," she said, "because there is another war to fight against poverty, disease and ignorance.

"We have promises to keep to our people of work, food, clothing and shelter, health and education.

"The weaker and underprivileged sections of our people—all those who require special measures of social security, have always been and will remain uppermost in my mind.

"Youth must have greater opportunity. The young people of India must recognize that they will get from their country tomorrow what they give her today. The nation expects them to aspire and to excel.

"The worlds of science and art, of thought and action beckon to them. There are new frontiers to cross, new horizons to reach and new goals to achieve.

"No matter what our religion, language or state, we are one nation and one people."

There was worldwide interest in the election of Indira Gandhi as Prime Minister of the world's largest democracy. The news captured headlines the world over. Letters and telegrams poured into New Delhi from all continents. One account says that at least 10,000 cables were received from friends and world leaders. Pope Paul sent a message of blessing. In his cable, President Lyndon B. Johnson wished her every success as she assumed leadership of the world's largest democracy: "The relations between our two countries are firmly grounded in our common dedication to the principles of human dignity, human welfare, democratic institutions and peace. Under your leadership, I look forward to broadening and deepening this community of interests and pledge our friendship and cooperation to this end.'' In a message of congratulations, the Soviet Prime Minister Kosygin said, ''In the Soviet Union you are greatly respected as India's prominent political figure and stateswoman and we are convinced that the government of India headed by you will follow along the road of Jawaharlal Nehru and realize his ideas.''

The Nehru family has always been blessed with many beautiful women. Beauty and brains have been a tremendous combination for the success of family members. This has been generally acknowledged, although some opponents of the Congress berated their participation in politics. Once, in an angry mood, Sir C.P. Ramaswami Iyer, the old Dewan (a chief minister appointed by the Maharaja), accused Nehru of exploiting the beauty of the women of his family for political advantage. The public never forgave him for this unwarranted and untruthful assault on their idol.

Commenting on the election of Indira, Mrs. Chester Bowles, wife of the American Ambassador to India, pointed out that, ''it was a unique thing that a woman and a young woman at that should be Prime Minister of the world's largest democracy.'' There was much gladness among the women of the world that one of their number had become the leader of five hundred million people. Naturally, they were proud that one of their number was on ''top of the world.'' In some quarters there were questions as to how the young lady would fare.

Men in general have a tendency to think of women as the "weaker sex."

Indira, a student of anthropology, knew better. Some anthropologists are of the view that women have natural superiority over men. In support of their arguments they say that women bear children, nurse, nurture and care for them; they have less diseases and live longer. They outlive men by an average of four or five years. More girl babies survive than boy babies. They are said to be stronger at birth than boy babies. Professor Montague, a distinguished scholar on the subject, points out that girls develop skills earlier than boys, such as buttoning and unbuttoning clothes. Another scholar, Dr. Beerstead, pointed out that men being jealous of women's physical superiority (especially in their ability to bear children) kept them under subjection through the ages and prevented them from participating in public activities that would develop their muscular strength. Sometimes they used to destroy women's capacity to bear children. In spite of age long subjugation, she has proved herself more intelligent than man, because she has survived by her wits in a man dominated society.

India has long become used to women in positions of leadership. The history of India is vibrant with the narratives of the leadership of heroines like the Rani of Jhansi, Chand Bibi and Tara Bai. In 1707, Tara Bai was the leader of the Marathas. She inspired in them such great courage, and was so skillful a leader herself, that she defeated the mighty Mogul Emperor Aurungzeb. The Marathas' power kept on growing until by 1757 two-thirds of India was free from Mogul rule, and in 1761 the Marathas occupied the government buildings at Delhi, the then capital of India.

Under Mahatma Gandhi's leadership women took a daringly active part in the freedom struggle. Every field of political work was wide open to them. In free India, women have occupied many positions of leadership. In fact, at the time of Indira's election there were no less than sixty women in Parliament. Women have served with distinction in the central cabinet and state ministries. A distinguished daughter of India served as President of the United Nations General Assembly. Several women have served as judges in the courts of the land. However, Indira made it clear at the very outset that she was going about her task, not as a woman, but as a human being. In answer to a question at a news conference, she said, "I do not regard myself as a woman in regard to the job. I am just an Indian citizen and the first servant of the land."

Indira was very clear about her task as Prime Minister. While addressing a mass meeting, at Choupatty Sands in Bombay City, she said, "I will tell you a story of Gautama the Buddha. Famine stalked the land and none of the rich grain merchants would come forward to help Lord Buddha feed the poor. Then a beggar-girl volunteered to collect the food grains for him. People laughed at her. But she calmly assured Lord Buddha that she would go round the houses, collect handfuls and distribute the stock so collected." Indira envisages herself as the girl in the story of the Buddha, who will secure the cooperation of those concerned to ensure a better future for the suffering masses.

Indira started functioning officially with a profound sense of dedication, "It is what might be called the most difficult job in the world." She found calm in the good perspective of India's long and eventful history, in terms of world history.

Her father, coming to India after many years of training in England and many friendly contacts with the west, had said that at times he felt more at home in the west than in India. The daughter, in spite of contacts with western institutions and ways of life, always felt at home in India. She was deeply rooted in India, its culture and traditions. She acknowledged that her deep loyalty and appreciation for India's cultural heritage came from her mother, Kamala Nehru. She gave a warm tribute to her mother in these words: "It is my mother whom I admire more than my father. He animates me to soar into the clouds; yet her memory acts as a sort of lever keeping me attuned to earth's solid hold."

She chose an eminent team of ministers to work with her, some (Gulzarilal Nanda, Home Minister; Choudhuri Chavan, Defense; Swaran Singh, External Affairs and Chagla, Education) were in Shastri's cabinet, and others (Asoka Mehta, Planning) were new recruits.

No doubt, Indira had brought new blood into the ministries by selecting several from the younger generation to serve as deputy ministers and parliamentary secretaries. This was indeed a corrective to the imbalance that had long existed, cabinets being filled in the past with elderly people (the average age being sixty and above). She always had a strong belief that youth has a vital contribution to make to the progress of a country and that it should be associated with every level of administration. She had often spoken of her awareness of the untapped resources of youthful manpower in the building of the nation. "In every sphere of activity, youth must be given the fullest opportunity. They must be inspired with a sense of involvement into the national development."

The Prime Minister set the pace for the cabinet. She was marked by the punctuality and dispatch with which she attended to her office work. There was a reasonable division of labor and responsibility. Her colleagues and subordinate officers had the opportunity to express their views and receive careful attention. Indira was known to examine files with record speed. She wanted to cut through the notorious jungle of bureaucratic red tape that slowed down the country's progress. It has been reported that she examined a bulky file (which ordinarily takes hours and days for disposal) in ten minutes and made the secretary in charge take immediate action. She checked back to make sure that the instruction was followed through. It has already been reported that Nehru was insistent about clearing his desk each day. But in his later years, perhaps because of limitation of physical strength, decisions were delayed and work slowed down.

His daughter faced her tasks head-on and managed to cut through a great deal of red tape. The curse of India is bureaucratic snag, clinging to a lot of officiousness that hurts and humiliates the people. Any leader who can end it will save the nation from downfall. During the writer's visit to the Prime

Minister's office, he quickly became aware of an atmosphere of earnestness and efficiency among the staff in attending to business. Indira seemed to command from her staff a special kind of respect blended with affection.

Nehru and Lal Bahadur used to let interview times telescope one into the other. They would not want to offend visitors by strict adherence to the time schedule. However, Indira managed to carry on the interviews on time without offense to the visitors. Perhaps she was too business-like. Many visitors report that they talked; but there was no communication. To some she appeared remote, cold, almost glacial. To a few she appeared impenetrable, aloof, mystifying, a very big question mark.

There appears to be a touch of vanity and self-consciousness in Indira, as is possible in a most lovely lady of many accomplishments. Those who do not know her background can easily misunderstand her during interviews. She sits and listens sometimes motionless. Other visitors are deeply discouraged by her reserve and the fact that her face does not show any expression, either of approval or disapproval of their representations. Others convey the impression that she froze up to get rid of them. They feel ill at ease and say she is too detached and austere. Some interviewers attribute this demeanor to aristocratic snobbishness or plain lack of interest in individual problems. Others complain that she snubbed them. One recommended that Indira read *How to Make Friends and Influence People.*

All these are superficial views. Only those who know the lonely and anguished life that she led as a child can understand. For years, when her parents were in jail or her father in jail and her mother on a sick bed, Indira lived in tragic loneliness. She experienced the constant despoliation of her house by the police. She witnessed the police harassment of her relatives. All this left a deep impression on the lonely child and, thus, she grew to be very reserved and forbearing in the process. Also, her life has been riddled with crises for which she has had to build her own shelter. A journalist who followed her life and work for years observed that "in moments of stress and tension, she silently withdraws to herself. Those who know her often notice the impenetrable barrier that separates her from others, but they forget the ordeals through which she has passed in her earlier days." The poignant experiences of early days have left their profound impression on Indira's personality. Jesus said: "By their fruits ye shall judge them." If the critics would judge Indira by this criterion, they would recognize that the lady is warm-hearted, compassionate and intensely interested in the problems of the individual, especially the poor and destitute. Who has done more for social service in India than Indira Gandhi? She is, among other things, the architect of the Social Welfare Board with its national network of social service organizations. It has brought help to almost every part of India.

Some critics of the Administration in New Delhi speak of the "Palace" with reference to Indira, as Americans speak of the White House when they discuss the President of the United States. The use of "Palace" in India has connotations of the high and mighty and the unapproachable. These connotations are absurd and irrelevant as far as Indira is concerned. Her residence at No. 1 Safdarjang Road is a modest one-story house. It is comfortably and tastefully furnished, but is far from anything of a palace. The occupant of the house might by nature be a quiet and reserved person. Yet, she relaxes in the company of relatives and friends and is known to be happiest when in the company of scientists, writers and artists. She has excelled any national leader in India, or anywhere in the world, in her generosity to keep open house for people every morning. Each morning she is at home to individuals and groups who come to visit her.

In some respects she has outdone her father in rapport with crowds. In the morning before leaving for office, Nehru used to allow time to meet some individuals and groups who waited for him at his residence. Indira perfected this tradition by having a morning session for an hour. She had a tent set up on the grounds of her residence to accommodate nearly 200 visitors. When there is an overflow crowd, the children sit on the carpet on the floor.

Just before leaving for her office, Indira comes to the tent with aides and visits with the individuals and groups. She moves about briskly. Several come just for darshan. (The word literally means sight, but connotes the tradition of seeing a great personage and receiving the satisfaction thereof.)

The writer was at the Prime Minister's residence early one morning to observe this procedure. Several persons were waiting in the living room as Indira came in with hands folded in namaskar (salutation). A painter-soldier from Kashmir, who painted as a hobby, came with a portrait of Indira and that of a youngster from the hills. He made a presentation of them to her. A photo of the scene was taken. Indira was brief and appreciative. She asked if he painted these. He said "yes." "I like the painting, but I do not like myself," was the modest reply of a proud lady. The soldier was exhilarated and satisfied. He had come several hundred miles to make the presentation. The meeting was worth every mile. There was an author who presented one book and several pamphlets. Indira received these courteously, thanked the author and gave them to an aide. Then she moved on to a young couple and was deeply in conversation with them for a few minutes. Soon she moved on to meet all the people waiting in the *Shamyana* (specially erected tent) on the grounds. The people saluted the Prime Minister, exchanged greetings and left. Some collected autographs. Others got photographed with her.

Many came from near as well as distant places to submit grievances directly to their Prime Minister. The aides accompanying her were asked to make note of grievances and take necessary action to redress them. Amazing as it would seem, at the end of the hour, Indira had visited with all the people gathered there. Some were ill clad, coming directly from the farms. Others were elegantly dressed businessmen and potentates. Also, there were many women and children eagerly waiting to see her.

This procedure of meeting the people directly is one of the best instances of democracy in the world. One of the aides told the writer that anyone would be able to see the Prime Minister. It was the truth. All manner of people, the humblest peasant as well as the turbaned chieftain could come. They all see their Prime Minister. On the day that the Chinese were shelling the Sikkim border, the writer was at the Prime Minister's residence and was amazed to note that, even on such a crucial day, the weary and worried leader took time out to visit with the people who gathered on the grounds. The grounds were covered with people; for instance the teachers and students of a school were there. The Prime Minister visited with them. Much might not be accomplished by hurried confrontations of this nature. So what? Much might not be expected by many except to see and have a word with their Prime Minister. Whatever the case, this is democracy in action. It is like an oasis in the howling desert of world politics.

Indira usually puts in a long day of sixteen hours of work. She rarely retires before midnight. It is a grueling ordeal which the young lady takes in stride. When the Parliament is in session, she has to spend most of the day and sometimes part of the night there, especially when very important matters are discussed. Although in practice the minister of the portfolio concerned is expected to answer questions from members of India's tumultuous Parliament, the Prime Minister sometimes has to go to the rescue of ministers being badly battered by "merciless interrogations." Evenings are generally taken up by Congress Party meetings, civic receptions to visiting dignitaries, state banquets and other official functions. Generally, the Prime Minister gets back to her residence by 9 p.m. Some people are usually waiting to see her and she has to attend to them with dispatch. After dinner, she works with her files till midnight in her bedroom and then "let the honeyed wings of sleep hover over her."

She often has to go on extensive tours within India or abroad. On tour her programs are usually extremely busy ones. Mr. M. Chalapathi Rau, distinguished editor of the *National Herald* and close friend of the Nehru family, records her program for September 19, 1966: "She flew in the morning to Patna, changed planes to go to Monghyr, addressed a public meeting of 250,000 people; returned to Patna for lunch; after which she drove to address the Rajendra Prasad Institute of Medicine at one end of the town and a group of 5,000 Congress workers at the other; then a public meeting of 500,-000 people and a speech to a small group of Youth Congress organizers; after which meetings with 22 separate delegations and memorialists; then dinner with the Governor and members of the Bihar Cabinet, followed by two hours of working at files. The next day she addressed three public meetings, traveling scores of dusty miles standing in open cars, and had a long talk with Acharya Vinoba Bhave, the exponent of Gandhian philosophy."

A major reason for the Prime Minister's long work day is the fact that problems have piled upon problems. Old Himalayan problems like poverty and food shortage were always there. It might be remembered that when Nehru was elected Prime Minister, a British journalist asked how many problems he had to face immediately. The answer came with swiftness, "four hundred million!" Since that time, the population of India has increased, and if the same question is put to Indira today it might be answered by the figure "five hundred million problems." To this one must add the problem of population explosion.

Sizing up the situation in the country, Indira pointed out that the troubles were due not to shortcomings in policy, but to delays or deficiencies in its implementation. Concerning the national programs, she noted that "There is a disconcerting gap between intention and action. To bridge this gap, we should boldly adopt whatever far-reaching changes in administration may be found necessary." To clear the jungle of bureaucratic red tape is one of those "far-reaching" changes required forthwith. But how?

Like former President Herbert Hoover in the United States, Indira came to the helm of the government while an economic crisis was building up. In both cases the crises were inherited by them, although the tendency of the public was to blame the incumbent leaders. Both received crowns-of-thorns pressed hard on the heads.

Pakistan's aggression in Kashmir and the consequent war during the previous autumn had caused heavy economic loss for India to the tune of two billion dollars, and had delayed its planned progress in agriculture and civilian industries. As a result of the war, aid-giving countries in some instances stopped their aid programs. Lack of resources led to reduction of industrial production.

To add to the miseries of the farmer, the rains failed. It has been reported that the monsoon of 1965 was the poorest in eighty years. It was estimated that the grain production for the year 1965-66 would be seventeen million tons less than the previous year. In other words, some 25 percent less than that of 1964-65.

The serious food shortage was felt especially in states like Kerala and West Bengal. The immediate task in January was to organize relief for areas where the first harvest failed and to have a well organized program of procurement and distribution of food. It was also necessary to prepare for intensive cultivation during the next season.

There was widespread unrest against the rise in prices of commodities like kerosene and the existence of black markets. Government employees like those of the Andhra government were threatening to quit work unless there was an increment in their earnings. The food problem was acute, especially in Kerala in the summer of 1965. To protest against the inadequate rice rations, a one-day bandh (stoppage of all work) was announced by most of the political parties of the state, including Indira's own Congress Party. The writer was an anxious witness of the bandh in Trivandrum, the capital of the state. Most of the work was stopped and the day ended in sporadic violence from one end of the state to the other. To hunger was added bloodshed.

Indira realized that something had to be done and soon. So, within hours of taking the oath of office, she sent urgent appeals to the Madras and Andhra States to rush rice consignments to Kerala on a top priority, emergency basis. On the same day, she announced that she would fly to Kerala to study the situation first-hand and reassure the people of the Centre's intentions. She could only make gestures of personal concern like these, but even a gesture has its usefulness. It is a token of action that must follow.

Indira appealed to the people to change their food habits by using more wheat and other cereals in the face of the rice shortage. She set the example by giving up rice from her own menu. Mahatma Gandhi used to say that a good example has the quality of multiplying itself. But the mood of India today is impatient and sarcastic. Some critics asked how one person's renunciation of rice could feed the millions of Kerala. But they failed to realize that the integrity of a culture lies in the practice of one's precepts. They also failed to realize how much Indira relished eating rice. The delicious combination of rice and curry (especially chicken and fish curry) is unbeatable. The people of Kerala consider this the most delectable dish in the whole world! Some people there would overthrow any ministry to make sure that they got their rice and curry! Some rice eaters would "rather fight than change."

Indira supported a program to import grain and fertilizer, and toured the scarcity areas of Orissa, Madhya Pradesh and Maharashtra. She was successful in getting state governments to start extensive relief works and food distribution arrangements. Furthermore, she gave massive support to a program of intensive cultivation.

Among the achievements in relieving food shortage, the following are especially notable. Nearly
fourteen million tons of grain secured both by
procurement in the country and by import from
the United States were distributed. To prevent
hoarding and black marketing, nearly 128,000 fair
price shops were established. Formal and informal
rationing brought fair distribution of food to nearly
116 million people. Free food was made available
to nearly seven million mothers, children, and the
aged and infirm. Also, about three million people
were provided with work and wages by means of
relief projects.

For some years a revolt had been brewing among
the Mizo tribesmen in Eastern India. These hill
people, numbering more than 260,000, resented their
being governed by the Assamese of the plains. They
showed their resentment by blocking roads, raiding
towns and attacking Indian Army patrols. Nehru
in his own conciliatory way offered the Mizoes a
plan by which they would be granted a measure of
local autonomy within the framework of the Indian
Constitution. However, the aggressive Mizo National
Front rejected this plan. They demanded complete
independence from India. When revolt flared up
early in 1966, Indira flew to the Mizo area and,
instead of merely threatening the rebels with military action, she broadcast a personal appeal to them.
Later she displayed the same combination of firmness and elasticity when, in response to widespread
resentment against the British peace workers'
partiality for the war-like Nagas, she ordered the
expulsion of Rev. Michael Scott. But she would

not bow to the clamor to end peace negotiations with the Nagas.

One of the perennially controversial issues that had been causing trouble for many years was the Sikhs' demand for the creation of a Punjabi-speaking state. With her characteristic sense of political realism, soon after her election Indira decided that the inevitable was also the desirable end. She put her weight on the side of the Punjabi Suba. Within a few weeks the government announced the decision to create a Punjabi-speaking state. The mass of the Sikhs were happy, but the Hindus, led by Jan Sangh, challenged the decision and held demonstrations that got out of control. In the town of Panipat, violence and homicide erupted and three Congressmen were burned alive by a mob. In the capital itself, the demonstrations led to a panic. Shops belonging to Sikhs were looted and burned. It was a testing-time for the new Prime Minister.

That day, over-riding the objections of her security staff, she not only toured the riot-torn area but also let it be known that action would be taken by the Home Ministry for any disturbance of the peace. She called the Jan Sangh leaders to a conference and conveyed a stern warning to them. Within forty-eight hours, life in Delhi was normal again.

In Parliament, Indira had fairly smooth sailing in the early days. The opposition was biding their time. The Congress Party had 392 seats in a 501 member Parliament. Thus, it was not too difficult to get the various government bills passed through Parliament.

As days passed, however, a number of things happened which threw the Parliament in continuous uproar. Among these were food shortages, rising prices, the establishment of fertilizer factories, the devaluation of the rupee and a ban on cow slaughter. Many began to compare Indira unfavorably with her father. Nehru's personality had dominated the Parliament as well as every gathering he went to. In Parliament he had the wit and wisdom to battle the most war-like opponents. He showed a finesse in Parliamentary debate which the intellectuals appreciated. In short, he had a personality that seemed to thrive in a fight.

Indira, who was not used to Parliamentary leadership, moved first with apparent self-consciousness and uncertain steps. However, nobody could miss the candor of her statements or the courage of her convictions. In due course, she became more sure of her steps and was well prepared to fight back whenever and wherever necessary. Her supporters became more confident that the young lady would survive the storms.

Perhaps Indira's greatest obstacle was a lack of rapport with the Congress hierarchy. The tactlessness and the lack of imagination of some of her associates contributed to this. Indira was blamed for not taking the Congress leadership into confidence in policy-making on important matters, such as the devaluation of the rupee and the fertilizer factories. A justification stated in her behalf was that she was asserting her independence as the Prime Minister of the people who is already committed to implement certain policies. Evidently, she did not want to be

a tool of party leaders. She felt that so long as
the policies to be followed were in the best interests
of the people she should go ahead and implement
them, even if the Congress leadership was not in
favor of them. Congress President Kamaraj was
so disappointed by some of the actions of the Prime
Minister that at one time when he was interviewed
on the subject of his working relationship with the
Executive, he slapped his head with both hands and
said, "I am a small man, who made a big mistake."
This was his dramatic way of expressing regret
for the part he played in the choice of Indira for
leadership.

In Bombay, she faced a stormy session of the
All-India Congress Committee. There were sharp
criticisms about agreements with the United States
concerning fertilizer factories, as well as the establishment of the U.S. Education Foundation. They
accused Indira of giving in to the United States
on aids which were alleged to have political strings
attached to them. She brushed the criticisms
aside as unfounded, and stood by her program of
encouraging U.S. investment for India's development and the implementation of the Fourth Five
Year Plan. After explaining the rectitude of her
position, she told them unequivocally that she was
ready to resign if they were dissatisfied with her
actions. Indira was at her best when there was
a fight on hand. She did not mince words. The
All-India Congress Committee was stunned by the
courage of her convictions and the candor of her
statements. Of course they wanted their leader to
continue. No doubt they expected that she would

be the greatest asset in general elections. They could not afford to drop her.

Although at odds with the Congress leadership, Indira still was the charismatic leader and chief "box office attraction" for the party. In fact, in the country as a whole, she drew larger crowds than any other leader. In spite of the seemingly endless torrents of criticism from the opposition parties, their demonstrations, strikes and walkouts, the mass of people still had a great love for Panditji's daughter. After all, Indira was a heroine of the freedom struggle. She came in the line of Gandhiji, Panditji and Shastriji; she gave of herself unselfishly for the welfare of the people and her sacrifices for the good of the country were many. Also, her great personal beauty and charm cannot be missed. So, wherever Indira went the masses gathered to pay respects. They waited for hours and hours just to see her. They showered flowers on her. She was profusely garlanded at meetings. But in a meaningful gesture, she generally gave the garlands back to the people. One of her aides said that often she would send the flowers she received to a children's colony in New Delhi. An eminent journalist spoke of her as a Prime Minister "who can crinkle the eyes, toss the sari draped coiffure and smile away momentarily at least the unbelievable cares and woes of the past and present."

Indira is dedicated to the promotion of friendly relations between India and other nations. She has a warm appreciation for America, where she had been an honored guest several times. She has also traveled widely in European and Asian countries.

Concerning contacts with other lands, she said that India has been "much benefited by contacts with foreign countries. Indeed, the life in the cities and amongst those educated abroad has been greatly influenced by what is happening in other lands. But, naturally, the ideas that we are taking over have to be adapted to the specific conditions prevailing here. The same thing applies to social welfare work. Most countries in Europe and America are well ahead of us in this field, but the problems they face are so different from ours that we cannot adopt any scheme exactly as it is from them. We have to formulate something of our own."

Two months after her election as Prime Minister, Indira undertook a journey of friendship to the United States. On her way to Washington, she met President De Gaulle in Paris. On her way back, she had meetings with British Prime Minister Harold Wilson and Chairman Alexei Kosygin of the Soviet Union. Some of her right-wing critics want her to get India aligned more closely with the United States for defense and economic aid. On the other hand, left-wing critics decry her for visits to the United States and the receiving of U.S. aid. They charge that by receiving aid, she is giving in to political domination by the United States. None of these criticisms can hold water because Indira, like her father, is dedicated to non-alignment and friendly relations with all nations. She does not see this world as divided into right and left. "I think," said Indira, "most of us are in the center. In a country like India, where the basic problem is one of poverty and of trying to convince the average man that you are on his side, you have to be more or less in the center and try and keep as many people with you as possible.''

One must provide for defense and the basic needs of the people, such as food, clothing and shelter. India was constrained to supplement its resources by means of aid from friendly nations. Several nations in the East-West power blocs rendered generous and timely aid. India has received more economic aid from the United States than from all the other countries put together. So far it has amounted to over $7,271 million. The aid between June 25, 1965 and September 15, 1966 alone totalled $1,124 million. This shows a greater flow of aid than any other similar period. Only 32.4 percent of American aid involves repayment in exchange. About 19.9 percent represents grant. The remaining 47.7 percent is in the form of loans repayable in rupees. A substantial portion of American aid has been used for projects devoted to production of food and other agricultural commodities.

CHAPTER IX

VISIT TO AMERICA

In spite of occasional misunderstandings and frictions, India and the United States have had a cordial relationship. This relationship was highlighted by Mrs. Gandhi's 1966 visit to the United States. In fact, the visit helped to further augment the friendly relationship between the two great democracies.

The 1966 visit calls to mind a statement once made by Rudyard Kipling: "East is east, west is west and never the twain shall meet." In many strange and wonderful ways East *has* met West, and the twain have been mutually benefited. The spiritual East and the technological West have aided, and are now aiding, each other to achieve greater benefits for all mankind.

India has always worked for peace. It is indeed remarkable that, in a land where there are great diversities of people and tongues, there is also so much religious tolerance and national unity. This pacifist attitude is deeply cultural. It is, therefore, not by accident that two great pacifist religions of the world had their inception in India — Hinduism and Buddhism.

In an age where communications between peoples and rapid transportation are practically universal, an age that has seen much trouble between nations and peoples, an age in which India's own security is under constant threat, India has cast her weight in the direction of concord between all nations and peoples. She now works on a level universal enough to embrace the whole of humanity.

In spite of occasional aberrations, India and her leaders have long cherished the goal of world peace. Mrs. Gandhi, while in the United States, reaffirmed her country's continued interest in and efforts for promoting this condition. She, also, reaffirmed the friendly relations existing between India and the United States.

"India can fully achieve her own goals only in a world free from strife. You have mentioned your interest in peace, Mr. President. We in India are greatly concerned about peace, for to us it is not only a question of an ideal but one of very practical necessity to give us time and opportunity to deal with those other problems and questions which you have mentioned; that is, to be able to develop our country, to give opportunity to our own people to stand on their feet, to deal with the many obstacles and difficulties which a longstanding poverty has imposed on us." These were the concerns of the Prime Minister. Yet, she never specifically asked for any financial aid.

The principal purpose of the Prime Minister's visit to the United States was to deepen the friendly relations already existing between the two countries. She sought to further the causes of the two greatest democracies on earth; to further those conditions so necessary for true human progress everywhere,

the eradication of ignorance and poverty wherever
the conditions exist. To do this, it is necessary for
the two countries to pool their efforts and resources;
one, with a material technology virtually unparalleled in the history of civilization; the other, posses-
sing a spiritual wisdom so old and universal that
it seems to have been the veritable mother of spiritu-
ality. America needs India, just as India needs
America. One important development of the Prime
Minister's visit was a proposal by the President
for the setting up of an Indo-American Foundation
to promote scientific learning.

The busy schedule of Mrs. Gandhi began with a
meeting with President Johnson and other top U.S.
Government officials at Washington, D. C., March
28-29, 1966. She exchanged greetings with President
Johnson on March 28. There was also an exchange
of toasts on the evening of March 28.

Among her other activities was an address to the
National Press Club in Washington on March 29
and the making of a video tape for the NBC program
"Meet the Press," which was broadcast on April
3. On March 29, she was present at a reception at
the Indian Embassy in honor of President and Mrs.
Johnson. At this reception, Mr. Johnson paid a unique compliment to Mrs. Gandhi, by deciding to stay
on for dinner.

While in Washington, Mrs. Gandhi placed a
wreath at the grave of President John F. Kennedy. She was in New York City from March 30 to
April 1, where she met with Mayor John V. Lind-
say. She later addressed about 800 American businessmen and industrialists at the Economic Club of

New York. At the New York State Theater of the Lincoln Center at Philharmonic Hall, she was presented with an impressionistic painting of a rose. On April 1, she left the United States.

That Mrs. Gandhi is vitally interested in continued good relations between India and the United States is evident in the exchange of greetings on March 28: "India and the United States cannot and should not take each other for granted or allow their relations to drift. As friends committed to common ideals, they can together make this world a better place in which to live." That India should be self-sufficient is evident from the speech Mrs. Gandhi made at the exchange of toasts on the evening of March 28: "India very definitely is on the move. Mr. President, the United States has given India valuable assistance in our struggle against poverty, against hunger, against ignorance, and against disease. We are grateful for this act of friendship. But we also know that our 'Great Society' must and can only rest securely on the quality and the extent of our own effort. . . ."

Concerning India's friendship with the United States, Mrs. Gandhi stated further that ". . .friendship with America is not a new thing for us. Those of us in India who have been involved with the struggle for freedom have known from our earliest days your own struggle here. We have been taught the words of your leaders, of your past great presidents, and, above all, we were linked in friendship because of the friendship which President Roosevelt showed us and the understanding which he showed during some of the most difficult days of our independence struggle. I have no doubt it was also this understanding and friendly advice given to the British Government which facilitated and accelerated our own freedom.''

That the failure of democracy in one nation may mean a similar failure in other countries occupied the thoughts of Mrs. Gandhi: ''. . .India's problems today are her own, but they are also the world's problems. India has a position in Asia which is an explosive position. India, if it is stable, united, democratic, I think can serve a great purpose. If India is not stable, or if there is chaos, if India fails, I think it is a failure of the whole democratic system. It is a failure of many of the values which you and I both hold dear. . . .''

The American public's reaction to Mrs. Gandhi's visit was for the most part enthusiastic. In a farewell address in April, before leaving New York, Mrs. Gandhi said: ''At this moment I am filled with the happiest memories of the wonderful reception I have enjoyed, the kindness, courtesy and affection shown me, and the deep sympathy for India and its immense problems among all Americans. I came to the United States in search of understanding and I know that I have found it in abundant measure.''

A genuine respect and love for India was expressed in numerous ways by Americans — from the decision of Mr. Johnson to remain for dinner at the reception in the Indian Embassy, to spontaneous expressions of goodwill from the people in all walks of life.

In the exchange of greetings, President Johnson said: ''You have long been aware, Madame Prime

Minister, of the fascination that Indian culture holds for Americans. This extends from the painters of the Ajanta Cave and the Akbar Court to your brilliant film producers of the present day. I venture to think that there is much about the United States that your students find equally interesting...."

In this contemporary age, India has her problems. What country hasn't? The time is here when East and West must come together for a pooling of ideas and efforts in the solving of the problems of both sections of the world. In what seemed an almost spontaneous gesture, the President of the United States proposed the establishment of an Indo-American Foundation for the exchange of resources and ideas. The Prime Minister of India accepted the proposal.

The American mass communications media was almost overwhelmingly favorable in its acknowledgement of the greatness of Mrs. Gandhi. *The New York Herald Tribune* echoed this sentiment, when it editorialized that Mrs. Gandhi left behind her "a captivated American population, official and unofficial. . .her visitors and audiences offered almost the same reaction. They voiced pleasant amazement at the fact that a beautiful and frail-looking lady was shouldering the responsibility of leading the world's largest democracy in times of political and economic crises."

It is characteristic of the leaders of the world's two greatest democracies, that they should not confine their discussions to their own respective countries, but to have the problems of the world in mind also. *The India News* (April 1, 1966) reported:

"During their discussions, President Johnson and Prime Minister Gandhi reviewed recent developments, in South and Southeast Asia in the context of the Universal desire of men and women everywhere to achieve peace that respects liberty, dignity and the pursuit of a better way of life."

It was not only the political society but also the man on the street who seemed to have formed a very favorable impression of the lovely lady from faraway India. In a recent trip to Washington, the writer listened to a taxi driver converse about India. Asked if he had heard about Mrs. Gandhi, he replied, "Of course, we all liked her visit." Then he proceeded to relate that she must have been great even at the age of thirteen to have been able to "organize young people for national work." He was referring to Indira's work as a girl of thirteen in organizing the children's brigade, the Vanar Sena or monkey brigade, which helped the freedom struggle. (This was in the early nineteen-thirties, when Mahatma Gandhi was leading the second civil disobedience movement for India's freedom from British rule.)

There were also voices of dissent and criticism. For instance, the *Chicago Tribune*, a giant in the news media, lashed out editorially: "It comes with little grace for Mrs. Gandhi to criticize U.S. Policy in the Vietnam War and at that even before she left our shores. Yet she did so on a television program a few days after her talk with the President.

"Nobody in this country has ever suggested that India should become a satellite of the U.S. But we can suggest that Indian economy might benefit if that country should discard its Socialist theories and pattern its economy after our private enterprise system.'' Some small town newspapers also joined in on generously advising Mrs. Gandhi as to how India should henceforth pattern its economy and international relations.

Her first visit to the United States was in 1949, and she had been here every year since 1960. But this last visit in 1966 was the most fruitful of them all.

India and America have a deeper unity than any military alliance or economic cooperation can effect. It is the unity of moral and spiritual principles, of democracy, of peace. The futures of the two countries are inextricably intertwined, whether they individually desire it or not. They can rise together; or they will fall together. The political and economic stability of India will directly contribute to the security of the United States and the world. A bulwark of democracy in Asia, India is the largest democratic country in the world. In spite of failures, it has exercised considerable influence in the past for world peace. If India falls to fascism or communism, it will shake the foundations of democracy in the United States and all the world. Poverty, hunger and consequent unrest are the preludes to the rise of fascism and communism.

Some critics of the U.S. Administration have been impatient with the aid being given to India because India did not always tow the line of American foreign policy. There will always be disagreements on some matters between great democracies such as India and America. But it will be short-sightedness and folly to prevent or cut short whatever America is able to give to India in her distress. Every dollar spent on India can be the most fruitful investment on a long-range basis for the cause of freedom and "peace on earth!"

If anything, Indo-American relations were happier as a result of Mrs. Gandhi's visit. However, at the same time it should be recognized that there can always be disagreement between two large democracies on certain matters of policy as well as programs. Yet, on basic democratic commitments, there can always be broad areas of agreement leading to mutual assistance and united efforts for world peace. Mr. Chester Bowles, who for many years served with great distinction as United States Ambassador to India, has written with characteristic perceptivity about the bright prospects of Indo-American relations in the following words:

"Different cultural backgrounds, different languages, experience and viewpoints often create barriers which can be broken down only by a vigorous effort at understanding and occasionally by some frank talk on both sides.

"This is especially true of democratic societies like those of India and the United States where everyone speaks his mind, not always with full regard for the consequences. In totalitarian nations, where governments are able to stifle criticism and public expression and thereby cover up differences, a *facade* of agreement can often be created which masks rather than solves the basic differences.

"Although there will always be some differences between India and America, the goals we have in common are vastly more important. Here in India I feel a deep realization of this fact; and it is rare that you meet an Indian visitor to the United States who does not sense in my own country a similar warmth of feeling among Americans for India.

"We deeply believe that a free, prosperous, and peaceful India is a primary requirement for a stable and free Asia and that a *democratic* India will constitute a long step forward toward a democratic and free world society. We also believe that the basic goodwill and mutual interest exist to achieve this objective.

"That is why we Americans have been helping India over the last 15 years; that is why we expect to continue our assistance.

"We are facing troubled times when all nations are dealing with complex and unfamiliar problems. Inevitably, we shall sometimes see this turbulent new world from somewhat different perspectives.

"But as we seek common ground, let us never forget that America and India are working for precisely the same objectives: the right to live in a free society, the right of each individual to a full measure of dignity and economic justice and the opportunity for all people to live in a peaceful world."

For those who want to see and understand India here is a word of wisdom from Mrs. Lyndon Johnson, after her visit to India in 1961: "To see India, you must visit the villages. To understand India you must read Tagore. But to know India you must have a teacher like Indira Gandhi. I was lucky because I had all three." Irrelevantly one might add that according to one journalist the two charming

ladies, Mrs. Gandhi and Mrs. Johnson, look similar
in their appearance. Mrs. Johnson went on to
say that it was easy for the President to have immediate rapport with the Prime Minister because he
was on the best of terms with a similar personality!

Soon after the Prime Minister left the United
States there was much criticism of her in administrative circles for her continued call to stop bombing
North Vietnam. President Johnson was greatly
disturbed that a nation that receives so much aid
from America could be so voluble in its criticism
of American policy in Vietnam. He was also upset
because Indira had called a meeting in New Delhi
with President Joseph Tito of Yugoslavia and
President Gamal Abdal Nasser of Egypt at the
same time that the Manila Conference was going
on. At the Manila Conference President Johnson
was attempting, in concert with leaders of nations
allied in the Vietnam War, to explain the aims of
the war to the world. Indira's meeting ran counter
to this program and snatched away some of the
headlines in the news media.

Much water has flowed under the bridge since
the Prime Minister called for a stop to the bombing
of North Vietnam. It must now be clear that history
was on the side of the young lady from New Delhi.
If the tall Texan in Washington, D.C. had paid
attention to what she said, thousands of innocent
lives and billions of dollars worth of resources
could have been saved.

CHAPTER X

GENERAL ELECTION

Indira's leadership in the General Election was vital. As her party's standard bearer, much was expected of her. She was the star of the Congress Party campaign. Although by nature somewhat reserved and retiring, she went all out to meet the people for the General Election. She campaigned vigorously, traveling from one end of the country to the other, addressing rallies and making roadside stops to talk with people. On an average, she put in eighteen hours a day campaigning and also attending to the day-to-day administrative chores of the Prime Minister.

It must be noted that only two security officers were accompanying her. However, the local police were always alerted to keep order in the areas she visited. Everywhere she is described as a tough campaigner. For instance, in Jaipur, capital of Rajasthan and centre of great power for the opposition Swatantra Party, Indira had a rough time. In her meetings, there was heckling and jeering, especially in the rear of the crowd. But Indira was undaunted. At one meeting, when the jeering persisted she shouted angrily, "I have accounts of the way the opposition has been conducting their cam-

paign. There is no use for your shouting. I am not
going to be cowed and I won't be put off. I'll finish
my speech and then I'll sit down."

In the state of Rajasthan, with its twenty-three
million people, the Congress Party is weak because of dissensions. The strongest opposition
is the Swatantra Party led by the glamorous
Maharani Gayatri Devi. Next in line is the aggresive
Jan Sangh, which appeals to Hindu communalism,
religious predilections and fanaticism. The opposition parties derided the Congress Administration as
"the government of the politician by the politician
for the politician." Party leaders were charged
with corruption. During the election campaign the
Rani of Gwalior kept on challenging the crowds:
"If you can point to one single honest minister in
this state, I will take back everything I have said."
And always the crowd shouted *"Sabh chor hain!"*
("They are all thieves.")

Indira spent two days in Rajasthan. The fast
pace of her campaign was typical of those hectic
days. She visited seven out of twenty-six districts,
addressing an average of five scheduled public
meetings per day, besides making scores of un-
scheduled stops at junctions and along the roads.
Sometimes she had to stop to greet the crowds who
came to present her with flower garlands. At other
times, she tossed the vast numbers of flower garlands that had accumulated in the car to the crowds.

As a practice, she dressed very simply, in a
khadar homespun sari with the end draped over
her hair, a sign of modesty in India. She also
wore warm woolen socks and moccasins. Standing

confidently before her audiences, she spoke without notes, firmly and in a friendly manner. The average audience ranged from fifty to sixty thousand. She usually assured the audience thus: "We're not worried about the election. We're going to win."

The Congress Party had become very unpopular in several states. A lady of deep insight, Indira could sense the temper of the crowds; yet, she stoically put up with insults in some instances. Perhaps she was most affected by the opposition of rural people to the Congress. There were cases in some meetings where the very mention of the name Congress brought such comments as *"Sabh chor hain"* (they are all thieves).

Generally the reception was good. But as may well be expected, there were several occasions of violent protests by opposition parties. One of them got out of hand and ended with a stone fracturing Indira's nose. It was at a campaign rally in Bhubaneswar, capital of the state of Orissa. When Indira appeared on the election platform, a chant arose from a student group of the opposition: "Indira, go back! Indira, go back!" All the same the Prime Minister went on with her speech. When she finished and sat down, a Congress Party colleague started speaking. The heckling, hooting crowd started throwing stones on the platform. Unable to contain herself any longer, Indira strode to the microphone and shouted: "Will you give your vote for such hooligans who throw stones?" The stones continued to come, and she was hit on the nose by a rock. Wiping the blood, she continued, "I am not worried about the success of the Congress

Party. I am agonized over your future and over the future of democracy in this country." Officials with outstretched arms tried to shield her from the shower of stones while she spoke for two minutes. The crowd did not know at first that she was hit. But when her nose started bleeding badly, she asked for some ice. None being available, she took a handkerchief from her handbag and wiped off the blood. Once again she showed the courage typical of Nehru and implemented his message to her, "Be brave and all the rest will follow."

The Prime Minister, with nose bleeding, was escorted from the meeting under a hail of stones. She was helped to a car and taken to the governor's residence, where first aid was given and her nose X-rayed. The medical examination showed injury to the mucous membrane in the right nostril, bruises on the left side of the upper lip and a loosened tooth. Soon after receiving medical attention, Indira was raring to press on with the campaign. However, the doctors insisted on her entering a hospital in New Delhi for a few days of rest.

She was, therefore, admitted to Willingdon Hospital in New Delhi. After two days of rest and medical care, she was released. When she emerged from the hospital with her face bandaged a crowd of thousands waiting outside cheered "Indira Zindabad." ("Long live Indira.") She was advised to rest for the next few days.

In spite of all the violent outbursts by the opposition, the Congress Party led by Indira clinched a majority. Indira's own election was secure. She won the parliamentary seat from the Rae Barely constituency by an overwhelming majority.

It may not be incorrect to say that the personal outrages experienced, especially the stone-throwing incident, aroused the sensibilities of a vast number and brought for Indira and the Congress Party some sympathy votes.

When such rowdyism manifests itself in an election campaign, thoughtful persons are bound to share Indira's agony "over the future of democracy in this country." In a democratically constituted country the opposition parties can always capture power by means of the ballot box. This is illustrated in an unforgettable manner by the communist opposition having been able to form a ministry in Kerala as early as 1957. But to use violence, and on a lady, is to undermine the nonviolent foundations of Indian democracy and prepare the way for dictatorship. It is also the negation of the most elemental "rules of the game" of politics and of life itself.

Chapter XI

THE SECOND TIME AROUND

Indira was unanimously re-elected leader of the Congress Parliament Party on March 12, 1967. Her name was proposed by Mr. Morarji Desai and seconded by Mr. Jagjivan Ram. The proceedings took place in the central hall of Parliament House. The election itself took only about four minutes and the entire meeting was over in half an hour. Announcement of the results by the Returning Officer, Mr. A. K. Sen, was greeted with cheers.

Brief speeches were made on the occasion by the Congress President Mr. Kamaraj, Mr. Morarji Desai and Mrs. Gandhi. All the leaders emphasized the supreme need of unity during the critical times. Although originally Mr. Desai had intended to contest the leadership election, a compromise settlement was made under which he would serve as the Deputy Premier.

The Congress President said that, in spite of the reverses suffered by the party in the elections, the basic policies and programs were sound; however, he concluded that there had been many shortcomings. The masses expected rapid improvement and changes. The Congress should be prepared to satisfy these demands.

Mr. Desai exhorted the gathering to pledge loyalty to their leader, who bore heavy responsibility. He pointed out that India was facing many difficulties, both nationally and internationally; therefore, the interests of the country should be reckoned above the interests of the party.

Mrs. Gandhi said that she was overwhelmed by the confidence placed in her by this unanimous election. She thanked Mr. Kamaraj and Mr. Desai for their contribution to the party's unity and emphasized that misunderstanding should be a thing of the past.

She continued by saying that no responsible person could indulge in spectacular statements. In the past, after independence, the country had made much progress. But problems had also been mounting and the demand was not only for good policy but for quick and efficient implementation of policies and for quick results. She assigned top priority to the solution of the problem of food shortage.

"We have to create conditions," she declared, "by which democratic functioning is strengthened. We have to work along with non-Congress governments wherever we feel they are in the right direction." In her judgment, the most important thing was that the party and government get in tune with the masses. If they retained this mass contact, they would be able to fulfill their goals.

She pointed out that since 1962 there had been only a five percent fluctuation in voting. She emphasized that the need of the hour was for unity and hard work.

Later in the day, Indira held an important meeting with the press. In answer to a correspondent's enquiry, she stated that there would be a review of party policies and programs from time to time. She felt that there was need for a constant review, especially at that time. Her government would take a new look at all aspects of policy. But in external relations there would be no change in the policy of non-alignment and peaceful co-existence.

It was announced from Rashtrapati Bhawan, New Delhi, March 12, that President Dr. S. Radhakrishnan had requested Mrs. Indira Gandhi to form the new government and submit the names of her cabinet colleagues. She then called on the President. Earlier she submitted to him the resignation of her Council of Ministers. President Radhakrishnan accepted the resignation and asked her to carry on until the new cabinet was appointed.

On March 13, Prime Minister Gandhi, Deputy Prime Minister Desai and twenty-eight other members were sworn in by President Radhakrishnan. It was a simple and highly impressive ceremony held in the glittering Asoka Hall of the Presidential House. The ceremony was attended by distinguished officials, some congressmen and journalists.

The cabinet has an impressive array of experienced men and experts in various fields. They are notable for inclusion of youth and "new blood" as Mrs. Gandhi puts it. Among the persons with considerable administrative experience are Morarji Desai, Y. B. Chavan, Swaran Singh, Jagjivan Ram, Satya Narayan Sinha, M. C. Chagla and Asoka Mehta. As for expertise, there are Dr. V.K.R.V. Rao, noted economist, Dr. Triguna Sen, Vice-Chancellor

of Benaras Hindu University, and Dr. S. Chandrasekhar, well-known demographer.

Next to the Prime Minister, the most important
position of responsibility is held by Mr. Desai,
Deputy Premier and Finance Minister. At the age
of seventy-one, Morarji Desai is still strong. He
keeps in good trim by daily yoga exercises between
5:00 and 5:30 a.m. and is noted for well-disciplined
dietary habits. Whatever the secret, he looks at
least twenty years younger than his age. Although
variously described by critics as the "Congress
Party Monk," the "man behind the iron mask"
and the "lotus with the steelstem," Morarji speaks
of himself as a "rightist." He once said: "I am a
rightist in the sense that I believe in doing right."

The opposition parties are already working in-
cessantly to wrest control from the ruling party.
Some have already announced that they would not
let the new Ministry complete its term of service.
Others have taken a vow to sack the Ministry within the year. They tried to make good the threat
with lightning swiftness by introducing the first no-
confidence motion in Parliament. Mrs. Gandhi's
ministry survived this onslaught by a vote of 257
to 162. The motion had been introduced by a leader
of the Jan Sangh Party to protest the imposition
of Presidential rule in Rajasthan State in the wake
of political riots. The opposition, besides charging
the government with murdering democracy, accused
the United States Central Intelligence Agency with
interference in the election. It was further charged
that the CIA subverted a youth group and also aided
in transporting Stalin's daughter to Switzerland
although she was seeking asylum in India.

One of the important opposition charges against the Prime Minister has been her reluctance to permit production of nuclear weapons in India. In the interests of peace, her government has backed proposals being discussed in Geneva for a treaty prohibiting the spread of nuclear weapons. On March 20, Mr. M.C. Chagla, Foreign Minister, stated in Parliament "that India now has decided to use our nuclear capacity and that the government, nevertheless, has decided to use our nuclear capability for peaceful purposes only." He was questioned whether it would be safe for India not to produce nuclear weapons, when its "enemy," Communist China, was rapidly assuming the status of a nuclear power. Chagla replied that India would consider its own security of paramount importance in contemplating whether to sign any treaty to block the further spread of nuclear weapons.

On a long-range view, Mrs. Gandhi is disposed to arrive at political solutions in the relationship between India and China, as well as to achieve durable peace in the world. She believes that this could be achieved only by building the nations in Asia and the developing world "around popular and forward-looking nationalist governments dedicated to fulfilling the aspirations of their people."

Emphasizing that India was fighting a battle against China in the crucial forum of Afro-Asia, which China had sought to usurp as a political launching pad and as a revolutionary substitute for the United Nations, the Prime Minister said, "India's contribution in this regard has earned little notice or thanks. But I venture to suggest that this is a contribution of high significance since it has the unique distinction of meeting China's challenge on the ground and plane of Peking's own choosing.

"India is fighting this battle through its devotion to the democratic ideal. India is fighting this battle through its perseverance in planned development and its struggle against poverty. India is militarily holding a 2,000 mile Himalayan frontier against China. India is also fighting this battle in the crucial forum of Afro-Asia which China has sought to usurp as a political launching pad and as a revolutionary substitute for the United Nations.

By nature and upbringing Indira has the make-up of a world citizen. In her own words she feels "perfectly at home everywhere, in all countries." Like her father, she is deeply concerned about international peace. She has traveled constantly in Asia, Africa, Europe and America in the interests of promoting goodwill and durable foundations for peace. As Prime Minister of India, she held a Summit meeting with non-aligned leaders such as Tito and Nasser, in New Delhi, to find a peaceful settlement in Vietnam. She wanted her country to make its contribution to the reduction of world tensions. However, she is not experienced in the maneuvering that many politicians do. As a matter of fact, she does not care for that kind of politics: "I am not a political person in the sense in which politics is known in the world," said Indira. "I am interested in world trends and what India can do, I am passionately interested in these things. I am not interested in group-making. If I want to do something, I could do some maneuvering, but I am not made that way. I feel by doing that I will be taking away from my personality.''

Many readers in America may dissent and say, ''Well, these statements sound good. But what about India's stand in the Middle East crises this year? Is it on the level? Has not India been siding with the Arabs? Has it done anything as a harmonizer or mediator? Has it scuttled its mission of world peace?''

In the days preceding the outbreak of conflict in June, 1967, Indian delegates endeavored both inside and outside the UN to help preserve peace in the Middle East by urging restraint on the part of all parties. They supported the Secretary General in his efforts to secure a respite during which quiet diplomacy could be used to resolve the crisis. These efforts failed and the lightning war raged in favor of Israel. Once the hostilities started, India joined with several other members of the Security Council in advocating an immediate cease-fire and withdrawal of all armed forces to the positions held prior to the outbreak of hostilities. Mr. Swaran Singh, leader of the Indian delegation to the 22nd Session of the UN General Assembly, has given the following explanation for his move and the stand taken by India. ''We did this because of our firm conviction that a cease-fire without a simultaneous call for a withdrawal of alien armed forces was not only contrary to the eminent practice of the United Nations but also against its fundamental principle of non-use of force in international relations and the principle that territorial gains should not be made through military conquest. The deliberations

of the Fifth Emergency Special Session, even
though inconclusive, have shown a near unanimity
among member nations on these fundamental principles. It is a matter of regret, therefore, that no
progress has been made in securing the withdrawal
of Israeli forces from occupied territories and in
bringing peace and security to the area. India firmly
urges that this impasse be broken. We must all realize that failure to find a solution for the problems of the Middle East would lead to even graver
threats to peace. It is our belief that the foundation
of lasting peace in this section of the world should
be built on certain basic and fundamental principles of the UN Charter, in particular those con-
tained in Article 2. First, there must be a complete
withdrawal of Israeli forces from Arab lands under
their occupation. Second, all states must respect
the territorial integrity and political independence
of one another in accordance with the UN Charter.
Third, all outstanding problems in the region should
be settled exclusively through peaceful means. Finally, the just rights of the Arab refugees must be
safeguarded. As the Secretary-General has reminded us, ''people everywhere, and this certainly
applies to Palestinian refugees, have a natural right
to be in their homeland and to have a future.''

Nothing seems to have tarnished the image of India in the West more than its part in the Middle
East crisis, and especially the high drama in the
United Nations. Most of the news media lashed out
on India's policy, which they interpreted as being on the side of the Arabs (intended to woo their
support in the continuing struggle with Pakistan)

and not exerted for a constructive solution to the problem. Whatever the extent of the confusion caused by the speeches of India's government representatives, Indira has made her position clear more than once and put forth considerable effort to find a lasting solution to the Middle East problem. In October, 1967, she toured East European countries, including Yugoslavia, Bulgaria, Poland and Rumania; earlier she visited Egypt and Ceylon. She discussed the Middle East problem with the leaders of each country she visited.

On October 17, 1967, she visited Rumania's oil town, Ploesti, and received a warm welcome. Later, while meeting with newsmen, she was asked if she thought that Israel had a right to exist. She replied, "Israel's right to exist has been accepted by the U.N., so I do not think any further comment is necessary." She added, "We have to face certain facts. The first fact is that regardless of what our views were earlier, at the time of creation of Israel and so on, once Israel has been accepted by the United Nations, and we were also a party to that, we cannot subscribe to the elimination of Israel as a state. But we are all interested in a solution which will be a lasting solution and which will not all the time be erupting, and that solution must be something equally acceptable to Arab nations."

In a sprawling administration involving scores of departments, thousands of civil servants and the problems of 500 million people, it is only natural that there be shortcomings of one kind or other. Some could arise from the misunderstanding by an administrator of the directives of policy makers, others from misunderstanding or misinterpretation of the constitution, and yet others from carelessness or prejudice. But each problem, wherever it takes place, or from whomsoever it arises, is blamed by the public on the Prime Minister as the elected leader of the administration. A stout heart and "tough hide" are needed to bear the "slings and arrows" of criticism.

During the writer's recent stay in India, he came to know of one of those instances of mistaken directives from the government which caused consternation among the Christian minority. Some clog in India's administration machinery put out a notification that, because some missionaries sided with the revolutionary Hill Tribes, all foreign missionaries should leave India when their visa period ended. This would affect more than 5,000 missionaries and their families, from many nations of the world, who work in educational, medical, social service, emergency relief and evangelical fields. As a group they are doing more humanitarian work in India than any other group of similar size. Their services have been greatly praised by such leaders as Mahatma Gandhi and Jawaharlal Nehru. Indira, herself, from childhood days has been well acquainted with the social service of missionaries in Allahabad and elsewhere.

Naturally, there was surprise and shock in India and abroad that, in a secular state which has guaranteed freedom of religion, such a ruling was ever made. Many protests went to the Prime Minister. Deputations led by Cardinal Gracias and other Christian leaders made representations. Mrs. Gandhi was quick to recognize what had happened. Evidently, the notification was a mistake in terms of constitutional law and the basic elements of jurisprudence. Mr. Chavan, the Home Minister, in a statement brought calm to the excited atmosphere by making it clear that the ruling would not affect the missionaries in general, but only the ones against whom there was complaint with regard to their involvement in the revolt of the Hill Tribes.

The results of the recent general election had proved that a considerable portion of the masses of India had been dissatisfied with the Congress administrations. Their votes were clearly equivalent to votes of non-confidence in at least eight states. The trend of opposition to Congress is mounting steadily and swiftly. (To continue the Congress administrations in the customary way may assure that with the next general election a coalition of opposition parties will dominate the country.)

On receiving the election returns, Mrs. Gandhi remarked philosophically, "we have proved to the world that we have a fair and free election. That is the whole idea of having a democracy." While we appreciate the serenity of the Prime Minister's words, we cannot miss the glaring fact that the Congress Party has taken a "terrific beating," and now, while licking its wounds, has to fight hard for survival. Mrs. Gandhi's own future as leader is in the balance. Her party, having beaten a no-confidence motion by a slim majority of twenty votes, is in the balance. Threats of defection from the Parliamentary Party are rumored and a defection of twenty members can put a coalition of opposi-

tion parties in power. Opposition leaders, such as
the militant Dr. Ram Manohar Lohia of the Sam-
yukta Socialist Party, predict impending change.
He and his colleagues in the opposition parties are
leaving no stones unturned to ensure the overthrow
of the Congress regime. Dr. Lohia holds the view
(according to a source close to the Socialist Party
hierarchy) that all this hero-worship of the Nehrus
has clouded the reasoning process of the people and
hurt their progress. Therefore, he wants an end
to the domination of Nehru family members in Indian politics.

Compared with the general run of national leaders, Indira is young. Her stewardship has been only
over a short period of time. Thus, it is difficult to
make an assessment of her career as one would that
of a Mrs. Roosevelt or a Madame Chiang Kai-shek.
But, as Wordsworth said, "The child is the father
of the man," and the young lady is a "chip off
the old block" with more dispatch and directness
of approach to problems than her father. She is on
the scene at a fateful time in history, when the
leadership of women is vital for world peace. Men
have made a sorry mess of the world. "Perhaps no
woman," said a *Time* editorial, "has ever assumed
such responsibility as now rests on the slender
shoulders of Nehru's attractive daughter."

Today India is a graveyard of Congress leaders.
As to how long Indira can hold her own amidst the
gathering storm is the big question. No democracy,
and less so India with its "five hundred million
problems," can afford the luxury of changing prime
ministers like worn clothes. They should be given

at least the minimum time needed to prove or dis-
prove themselves, that is, to carry out their plans
or in the process be found wanting.

If a dissident faction within the Congress bolts,
it could easily lead to the overthrow of Indira's
ministry. The fall of this administration would probably, at least temporarily, create chaotic conditions.

The capability of the widely divergent opposi-
tions to consolidate their forces to form a ministry
at the center is a big question mark. And yet, the
democratic institutions have demonstrated a dur-
ability and resilience which shows definite hope.
Some observers see potential benefits from the
surprising election returns. A democratic student of
the Indian scene voiced the sentiments of the opposition leaders when he said: "The Congress Party
needed to be jabbed this way. It had grown fat and
flabby in office. This election shows a new dis-
crimination and sophistication on the part of Indian voters—it's a sign of vigor in the democracy."
"At the same time," he continued, "when you tear
down an old edifice—well, you do have moments of
doubt if the bricks and mortar for the new one have
not yet been delivered."

The opposition parties, ranging from communists
on the left to extreme conservatives on the right,
managed to maintain an effective united front during the election and afterwards. The Congress Party
lost control of eight of India's sixteen provinces.
For the first time, a majority of the Indian people
are living under non-Congress governments in the
states.

The unity of opposition parties was weakened, however, in the May (1967) presidential election in which the Congress candidate, Dr. Zakir Hussain, easily defeated the opposition candidate, former Chief Justice, Koka Subba Rao; thus, he was distinguished as the first Moslem, a member of a minority group, to become the august President of India. This was a personal victory for Mrs. Gandhi, who strongly backed the candidacy of Dr. Hussain. It was also a triumph for secularism in India's democracy. Dr. Hussain, a pioneering leader in Indian education, has brilliantly served India in many capacities.*

Teaming up with the President is the newly elected Vice-President, Varahagiri Venkata Giri, from the ranks of successful labor leadership. He has behind him an illustrious record of national service.

While traveling in India in the summer of 1967, the writer often heard the view expressed in many quarters that the present ministry was weak and that it would not last another year. Such a prediction was followed by a corollary that a coalition of opposition parties would rule at the center. Perhaps the most articulate exponent of this view was the brilliant Chakravarti Rajagopalachari, one-time pillar of the Congress Party and former Governor General of India. During an interview with Joseph Levyveld of the *New York Times,* Mr. Rajagopalachari pointed out that the new government that was sworn in in New Delhi (on March 13, 1966) would collapse and would be replaced by an alliance of opposition parties in about a year. He considered

---

* As this book goes to press, it has been learned that President Hussain has died of heart failure.

the administration of Mrs. Gandhi a "sickly care-
taker government," which would give way as soon
as the opposition parties were ready to replace it.

A leading nationalist daily newspaper of India
noted that Mr. Rajagopalachari, (now in his 98th
year), was still working with unparalleled zeal to
achieve his object of liquidating the Congress. The
strategy he pressed in his home state of Madras
was a united front of seven parties. Together they
swept the Congress Party from power. Today, he
is mapping the same strategy for a united front of
opposition parties to remove the Congress Party
from power at the center. He is certain that the
Congress cannot revive after its recent setbacks
because it has "become a party of careerists. It is
ideologically stuck in the mire of inflation."

Mr. Rajagopalachari wants a new government
which would lead to the abandonment of the heavy
state investment in industry. On the other hand,
he believes that there are many projects (such as
housing, water supply, and drainage system) which
can provide jobs for the people and thus make an
immediate difference in their lives. To him a sound
fiscal policy should be based on frugality and
practicality. He expressed the view that all the
parties, except the communists, will find they can
join together in support of his economic program.

Thus, something very strange is happening to the
politics of India, the land of contradictions. Accommodation has become the password. Opposition
parties, ranging all the way from the extreme right-
wing Jan Sangh and the extreme left-wing communist party, are working together, united not by

principles, but by the common goals of capturing and holding political power in the states as well as in the center. To some extent they are succeeding in the states of Kerala and West Bengal. There seems to be an understanding in the Kerala ministry (a united front of seven parties) to emphasize common goals and to submerge differences. For instance, the Chief Minister, E.M.S. Namboodiripad, and his party (which has the largest single majority in the legislature) are dominant in Kerala. And yet, the administration does not advertise communist principles and programs.

Similarly, the right-wing Muslim League speaks only very softly when it comes to communal matters. All told, there seems to be a working relationship among the parties which stresses the general goals for the good of the people and minimizes the particular theories and programs of the parties concerned. Evidently, there are two possible developments arising out of these. One is that after a while the parties concerned will become dissatisfied with their leaders, as a result of the lack of progress of their own brand of programs, and that the ministries might then go to pieces. The other possibility is that as a result of working together, the opposition parties will become more tolerant of each other and more responsible. Out of these coalitions will arise united opposition parties with a consensus of national and state goals. They can provide democratic alternatives to the Congress Party to administer the center and the states. A big question mark concerns the communist party of India (Marxist). Since they have a pro-Peking record, many responsible statesmen in India are worried as to the future of states dominated by them in the event of a conflict between India and China. There has been considerable relief of anxiety in this area because of the non-partisan manner in which Mr. E.M.S. Namboodiripad has handled some affairs of Kerala.

The angry mood of the country is reflected in the atmosphere of Parliament. Tempers often flare. The sessions at times become tumultuous. Business transactions are often delayed because of long-winded speeches and recriminations. All this, of course, is part of the warp and woof of democratic processes. However, one would like to see less heat and more light in a house that legislates for a nation of 500 million. The charismatic personality of Nehru commanded respect in Parliament. Generally, they would pay attention to him. When the sessions became stormy, he would bring some calm by his dexterous performance as a parliamentarian. Even when he spoke at length in monotones, they listened to his expatiation of theories. Indian intellectuals like elaborate exposition of ideas and ideals. Indira, on the other hand, is business-like, brief and to the point. They are not satisfied. They think she is too brief and sometimes incoherent or reticent. Several of their expressions in Parliament appeared to be too boisterous. Some of them might benefit by a few lessons in chivalry and decorum. They often pressure Indira with their demands. If she does not yield, some threaten to bolt the party and worse.

A major cause of the discontent is the food problem which has plagued Indira's administration ever since its inception. Soon after the Indo-

Pakistan War, an effort was made by President Johnson to secure a community of nations, along with the United States, to commit themselves to provide aid to meet the food shortage in India. While this was strongly criticized by some individuals and agencies as a veiled effort to deny increased aid from the United States, the principle behind this move is of vital significance to the future of starving millions in India and elsewhere. In a civilized world it is the duty of the community of nations to aid the developing nations so that the basic needs of its people in terms of food, clothing, shelter and education can be provided. It is especially important that there should be a global organization to meet emergency food needs and to combat famine conditions wherever and in whatever circumstances they arise. The Food and Agriculture Organization within the U.N., if operated under better conditions, could have been useful for this purpose.

But, as long as the U.N. and its agencies are kept enfeebled as they are today, leading nations such as the United States and the Soviet Union should take the initiative to organize the necessary world food reserve. This would ensure an abundance of food and the possibilities of surplus production so that millions of men, women and children in developing nations would not die of malnutrition or starvation. It is a tragic comment on our generation that each day nearly ten thousand people in the underdeveloped countries die as a result of illness caused by malnutrition. Of every twenty children born in these countries, ten are likely to perish in infancy

from hunger or from the effects of improper diet.
Another seven may suffer physical or mental re-
tardation. It is shocking to realize that half the
world's people experience chronic hunger or serious
deficiency in food. It has been contended that there
is a food shortage in some countries all the time.
But the difference between the present and the past
is that today we have the technological capacity for
expanded production of food to take care of the
needs of all peoples. Today the sufferings of the
poor are the result not of lack of know-how or
resources in the world but of lack of concern and
cooperative effort among the nations. It should be
recognized that no country in the world helps feed
the under-fed people of the world more than the
United States. Yet, there are millions of acres of
land in the United States that are lying fallow due
to governmental restrictions, whereas they could be
producing food to feed the starving millions. The
quantity of food that is wasted or thrown in the
garbage cans daily in the United States is sufficient
to keep alive nearly 365 million people throughout
the world who are dying annually due to illness
caused by malnutrition.

It is too early to make an adequate estimate of
the calibre of Mrs. Gandhi's administration. She
needs more time to carry out her programs. Whatever the future might be, Nehru's daughter has tried
sincerely to do her best for her country. Yet it
appears that her best has not been good enough. But
how could it be, when faced with the problems
of 500 million people? During her stewardship,
there was and is a food shortage. One might say

that India has always had a food shortage, especially after great floods and droughts which destroy
the crops. But these excuses will not be accepted
today in a free India with "rising expectations."
The demand is harsh and insistent: "Give us food,
or get out of office!" The old hero worship is
"gone with the wind." Leaders who do not "deliver
the goods" fall under the blows of public criticism.
Some are even manhandled. Dharna (sit down
hunger strike) and Gheraos (the demonstrators
circle a leader for hours so that he cannot move)
are resorted to at the drop of a hat.

Time is of the essence today. Unless the government of India moves with lightning speed to feed
the hungry millions and to eradicate poverty, the
country would be an easy prey for totalitarian communism as in China or military dictatorship like
Pakistan.

There is a shortage of food. But it is more true
and perilous that there is a shortage of "spirit,"
of enthusiasm, of hopeful, positive attitude that
"we shall overcome." There is a wave of skepti-
cism which is the bane of constructive programs.
Many disgruntled elements look for a military
dictatorship as the panacea for the ills of the land!
Mrs. Gandhi is well aware of these problems. At
a recent meeting in Bombay she recalled the events
which followed the All-India Congress Committee
session (at which the Quit India Resolution was
passed) twenty-five years before, and the spirit with
which people fought for freedom. She said, "we
are in need of the same spirit and courage to fight
the problems facing the country today. Our inde-

pendence will not be complete unless we meet the primary needs for the people." She called upon the people to resolve not to halt for a moment on the path to progress. Naturally, the scapegoat for all of India's troubles, especially food shortage, is the central government. Asked as to what steps the opposition could outline for the Prime Minister to relieve food shortage, an opposition leader said "she could resign. That is the best thing she could do for the country." But he, like many others, was not able to suggest a second choice. The fair lady towers high like a Mount Everest in her inscrutability, stubbornness and incorruptibility.

The present ministry can solve the problem of food shortage if it will mobilize the human and natural resources of the country for this purpose. In spite of the adverse effects caused by floods and droughts over a two-year period, it is still possible for India to become self-sufficient in supplying the food needs of its people within the next five years. There are a number of practical ways in which food production can be increased.

As a first step, several million acres which are not now under cultivation can be made cultivable by means of irrigation. Secondly, the millions of acres that now yield only one crop can be prepared for two or three crops annually. Thirdly, scientific agriculture (with the use of tractors, better seeds, fertilizers and pesticides) can greatly increase the food crops. Fourthly, the seas which border the Indian peninsula can provide a vast quantity of fish and other sea foods by more organized and mechanized forms of fishing with the use of trawlers and other sea crafts. Fifthly, there should be a well organized program of procurement and distribution of food. Sixthly, one cannot overemphasize the need for urgent measures to eliminate rats and other pests, which consume more than one-tenth of the crops of India. An Indian economist expressed the view that the food consumed by the rats and other pests in 1967 would have been quite sufficient to prevent the food shortage!

Along with an all-out effort at increasing food production, there should be a concrete effort at mass education of the people, especially in rural areas, to bring about a change in the unhealthy, traditional food habits. For instance, in a state like Kerala, rice is traditionally the staple fare. If other cereals, such as wheat, maize and millets, high protein grains, legumes and other protein-containing food (milk and milk products) would be accepted for the daily fare, much of the recurring food problem could be solved. While rice is in short supply in Kerala, there are equally nourishing or desirable foods grown in the state, such as bananas, mangoes and tender coconuts. (One coconut is reported to contain all the vitamin requirements a person needs in one day.)

There should be a national mobilization of personnel and material resources to solve the food production problem. Since this is an extraordinary emergency in the country, extraordinary measures should be adopted. Among the personnel resources which should be used on a part-time basis are the armed forces, the student body and the bureaucracy. Of course, the millions of unemployed can be employed on a full-time basis. As far as material resources are concerned, the top priority should be given to food production. Besides the money available from taxes and foreign aid, funds should be raised within India by floating an agricultural loan or by means of savings bonds earmarked for this purpose.

Food has become a weapon not of friendship but of politics, not of peace but war. Shakespeare spoke of the quality of mercy as "twice blessed" in the sense that "it blesseth him that gives and him that receives." But today giving has become a curse in many instances, especially to him that receives. The strings attached to giving require the receiver to side with the giver in his own plans of power politics and world domination. It is tragic that some countries that should speak for peace have been silenced by their economic dependence.

As far as India is concerned, if it is to play in any full measure its role as a mediator and harmonizer of conflicting nations, it has to become independent in its economy. The earlier India builds self-reliance, the sooner it will become a great power for peace. Meanwhile, the developed nations can make a lasting contribution to peace by sharing their mighty food resources with the starving peoples of the world.

Population explosion is a problem that has contributed to poverty and food shortage. Of course, this would not be the case if there were commensurate economic progress and increased production of food. Since the economists and demographers arrived at the conclusion that economic progress could not keep pace with the rate of increase of population, they have advocated family planning programs.

In 1961, the population of India was 439 million; the present population is estimated at 510 million and it is currently increasing at the rate of almost one million a month. It is expected to be 630 million by 1975 and a billion by 1991. The spectacular increase in population has been the result of a drastic fall in mortality rates; *e.g.*, the birth and death rates in the decade 1921-31 were respectively 50.8 percent and 40.4 percent; at present they are respectively 39.36 and 16.32. Life expectancy has increased from about 27 to 49.2 percent in the same period. This is the result of the far-reaching public health and medical relief measures undertaken since 1947.

The birth rate is relatively high, and a substantial part of India's development effort is absorbed by the increase of population; *e.g.*, though India's national income has increased during the last fifteen years by 68 percent, per capita income has gone up only by 29 percent. Similarly, the production of food grains increased by about 68 percent during the same period, but the per capita availability for indigenous production has increased by only 18 percent.

Circumstances constrain India to take the fullest measures both to raise productivity and to improve the diet at the same time. And it must promote programs by which the population could be stabilized. Education and a higher standard of living will play an important part in the achievement of these goals.

India's top health officials met on June 3, 1967 to seek a new way to slow down the country's rampaging population growth. The Health and Family Planning Minister, Sushila Nayar, warned that overpopulation might be "the most serious crisis" facing India. Delegates offered a variety of suggestions for eradicating the problem. They included compulsory sterilization for husbands or wives with at least three children; facilities in jails for sterilization of convicts who have at least three children, with a reduction in the prison sentence by fifteen days for having the operation; raising the minimum marriage age for women from sixteen to twenty-one; free distribution of contraceptives to all persons who want them regardless of their income; a cash allowance of $19 for all women undergoing the sterilization operation.

Of the various suggestions which were put forth at a meeting of the Central Family Planning Council, raising the marriage age for women seemed to have the best chance of eventually being approved by the Health Ministry and being submitted to Parliament for legislative enactment.

One official held out little prospect of the adoption of compulsory sterilization. "In a democracy like ours," he said, "we are opposed to making such an operation compulsory. We prefer to educate people on the subject and let them make their own decision."

The fifty-member Family Planning Council, which is composed of state health ministers, selected members of Parliament and leading doctors and sociologists, is considered one of the main co-ordinating groups in the nationwide drive to reduce the annual birth rate from 40 per 1,000 to 25 per 1,000 by 1971.

India's new Health Minister and a leading demographer, Sripati Chandrasekhar, has offered simple attractions to the citizens of India to join the family planning programs. For instance, he advertised the offer of a transistor radio to every man in the village who would undergo a sterilization operation. Humorists in India and abroad pounced upon it. They teased the Health Minister by insinuating that he is encouraging men to keep the company of the transistor radios instead of their wives. One comedian pointed out that it is easy to carry the radios around. However, the health minister is sincere and dead serious about the whole business. Large consignments of Japanese radios have been ordered for this purpose. The manufacture of transistor radios in India is also being pushed. In some places, the government has expressed its appreciation to the men who submit themselves to sterilization by giving a bonus of twenty-one rupees (a little less than three dollars). As the population has been increasing by a million a month the Health Minister had to campaign for more stringent measures. For instance, he advocated compulsory sterilization of all men who had fathered three or more children. The rationale behind this drive, as given by an authoritative source, is that it is far more humane for a man to be sterilized than be permitted to procreate a clan of children to walk the streets homeless and hungry! It was reported that chief ministers of several states supported this project.

But the latest report from New Delhi is that Mrs. Gandhi has turned thumbs down on it. The indefatigable Dr. Chandrasekhar has now come up with programs aimed at raising the minimum age for marriage of girls; and these will probably have less controversy and more practicality in the present context.

India's Health Minister hopes to stabilize the population at 700 million in the next decade by checking the rate of growth. He has pursued family planning very vigorously on an emergency basis. Yet, he confesses, "we are in a hurry and we have no time to lose. We have to run even before we have learned to walk, or else we will have to be going round the world with a begging bowl ad infinitum."

Latest reports indicate that the furor over the unorthodox methods of birth control and the aggressive Madison Avenue manner in which they were advocated have led to the government's relieving the very distinguished minister of his control and appointing the eminent political leader, and less aggressive advocate of family planning, Mr. Satya Narain Sinha, as Minister of Health and Planning.

It should be noted here that India's half billion people, who constitute 14 percent of the world's population, must gain their support from only 2.4 percent of the total land area. There is a large gap between the birth rate of nearly 40 per 1,000 and the death rate of almost 17 per 1,000.

Family planning has an interesting record in India. The Mysore Government opened the world's first government birth control clinic in 1930. In 1935, the Indian National Congress set up a National

Planning Committee and, in 1936, Mrs. Margaret
Sanger lectured to the All-India Women's Confer-
ence. Dr. Abraham Stone, the Planned Parenthood
expert, was sent to India in the early '50's by the
World Health Organization and the services of Dr.
Frank Notestein and Dr. Leona Baumgartner were
contributed by the Population Council. Dr. Frank
Notestein later became the Population Council's
President.

In 1955, a national program started to emerge
which has developed into a powerful federal structure composed of a Ministry of Health and Family
Planning, headed by Dr. Sushila Nayar; a commissioner, Dr. (Lieut. Gen.) S.P. Bhatia; and a Central Planning Family Institute, directed by Dr.
(Lieut. Col.) B.L. Raina. The rupee equivalent of
$210,000,000 has been provided by India's fourth
Five Year Plan for family planning. American
organizations such as the Ford Foundation, the
Rockefeller Foundation and the Population Council
contributed money and personnel, including biology laboratory workers and physicians.

Bombay has nearly reached the ten-year goal
of reducing the birth rate to 25 per 1,000. By May,
1967, about 900,000 Indian women visited 3,500
family planning centers and had been fitted with
intrauterine devices (IUD's). Also, more than
500,000 male sterilization operations were performed
in 1966, and a cumulative figure of 1,500,000 was
reached by April, 1966. The latest report indicates
that there have been 17 million loop insertions in
the two years, 1965-67.

Medical authorities feel that these two methods

are the best hope for reducing the birth rate. Earlier usage of the rhythm system, condoms, coitus interruptus, diaphragms, jellies and foam tablets was disappointing. Even though oral progestins, when taken faithfully, are more perfect for prevention of conception than any other contraceptive, it is felt that IUD's will prove best for mitigating India's population explosion.

IUD's are inexpensive (8.3 cents per unit), easily produced (a whole country can be supplied by a small factory run by fourteen technicians), remarkably effective and permanent for as long as desirable. Most Indian women prefer to be treated by women, but there are only 12,500 women physicians in India. Although most of the problems, such as pain from cramps, vaginal bleeding and pelvic inflammatory disease are rare and seldom disabling, there is still the problem of expulsion—a troublesome experience which most often happens during the first months after insertion.

Proper examination of patients is one of the keys to the successfulness of intrauterine contraception. The government realizes that IUD's and vasectomies are not the whole answer. So it has arranged to import condoms (while domestic manufacturing facilities are being expanded).

The "ideal Indian family" as advertised consists of 2-3 children with a birth spacing of 3-8 years. There is a highly organized effort to educate the people in family planning. Eighty-three medical colleges and 228 nursing schools have various training programs. There are men and women leaders for every village or group of 1,000 population. An auxiliary nurse-midwife and male health worker are scheduled for every 10,000 and a family planning health assistant for each 20,000. The government of India is spending forty million dollars a year on family planning programs. Two major goals to be fulfilled over the next decade are the insertion of 50 million loops and the performance of 12 million male sterilizations.

A number of Indian universities are doing research in reproductive biology (grants were given by the Ford Foundation). Important to the population explosion is India's animal problem. Some religious teachings forbid the killing of any living thing. Elephants, stray dogs and cows are eating the food that the Indian people need. Forestry officials assigned to Uttar Pradesh (the most populous state) suggested studies for the control of elephant births. Uttar Pradesh has chronic food shortage. IUD's have already been developed on an experimental basis for cows and dogs. This is the beginning of more to come. Discussions are going on about ways of dealing with the rats and birds also; together they are said to consume nearly 15 percent of India's food grains.

Population control and family planning are sensitive subjects and require the establishment of a new tradition of self-discipline, plus a fairly high living standard. Indeed, no developed country now has a birth rate above 30 per 1,000. At the same time, various study projects have indicated that many people in the underdeveloped areas are eager to learn about birth control, thus implying the importance of the technical know-how.

There is some criticism in the country about the use of methods for birth control. Critics point out that this will cause confusion and undue expenditure. A distinguished writer, Chanchal Sarkar, has said, "Today, the loop, tomorrow the injection, the next day an oral pill, or vasectomy, or tubectomy, the rhythm method, legalized abortions and so on. If it is the loop, there must be doctors to insert them; if it is sterilization there must be hospital beds; if the rhythm method, then propaganda is the main weapon. Has the government computed the cost of offering all these methods simultaneously?"

There is opposition to the program of birth control from many quarters. Muslims and Catholics consider the program unacceptable in relation to their religious beliefs. Some Hindu organizations oppose the program because they fear that lack of cooperation from Muslims and Catholics would in time reduce the present Hindu majority of 80 percent to a minority position. The illiterate villager looks at it with suspicion. And since the increase of children in general was considered a blessing, any attempt to prevent it might be considered as accursed. There have been instances in which villagers with long sticks attacked workers of the family planning program and drove them out. There are also very serious objections about the use of male doctors in providing birth control devices.

Some thinkers in India believe that the birth control program, in spite of all the expertise and expeditiousness, is not making any substantial dent on the population problem. It has not, according to these critics, brought any noticeable relief to problems like food shortage. They argue that India can, if its resources are developed, feed, clothe and house its population. They ask that a crash program be directed for the development of resources and not for the prevention of the birth of future citizens. If China could support 700 million people, why not free India its 500 million? Why should 40 million dollars be spent annually for birth control when that amount could be used to feed the children who are dying of malnutrition? The argument goes on. One side predicates its case on theory that the reduction of mouths to feed by birth control will provide more food for the ones already born. The other side waxes eloquent on the theory that in the overwhelming majority of nations of the world, education and improvement of living standards have brought about stabilization of population. They point, for example, to Japan, Taiwan, South Korea, Russia and countries of Europe and North America. In these countries there was no need for any crash program in birth control under the sponsorship of governments.

Today the land is reeking with real as well as imaginary discontent. Some propaganda has had such a resounding effect that law and order has become problematic. The nation's youth, and especially high school and college students, are restless. All manner of disgruntled groups start agitations—strikes, closing down shops, blocking transportation, communications, etc. There is growing fear of a possible communist take-over. Yet the Prime Minister maintains her calm amidst the gathering storm and declares that she does not fear such an eventuality.

India is desperately in need of a renaissance, a renewal of spirit, a new resolve and hope to build a happy and prosperous future as envisaged by Nehru. Through self-reliance and industry, India has to achieve the resources to feed, clothe, house and educate the helpless millions, so that as Gandhi desired, "every tear can be wiped from every eye." India has enjoyed prosperity in its golden age of great leaders like Asoka and Akbar. Why not now and more so? The new generation with the light of hope in their eyes, the flame of freedom in their hearts, with faith in the future, with united effort can make the desert bloom as the rose and turn India into a land flowing with "milk and honey." But where is the Moses who can lead the people from the dreary desert promise to the land of Canaan? Many still look with hope to Indira Priyadarshini Gandhi. Can she? Will she? If she will she can.

Parties and personalities pass away; but, the human race persists. By the turn of the century the population of the world will have doubled. As for India, it will have a billion people to feed, house and educate. These are problems that no one party can adequately solve. It requires the cooperation and united effort of all parties. It also requires international cooperation.

A consensus should be built up in the country about basic goals of progress for which all parties can work together. Every party, whatever its present name or form, can make a contribution to the welfare of India. Each party must place the vital interests of the masses above doctrines, formulas and dogmas (so many of which have already been discarded in other progressive countries). In a modern India the age-old prejudices and superstitions have no place. A Gangetic flood of rational thought and secularism should wipe out the mounts of superstition and communalism. The people must unite. Only they can build their future. The government can only help. The new generation with "flame of freedom in their hearts and light of knowledge in their eyes" should dedicate themselves to building the new India. There are unlimited possibilities for a determined, purposeful and "angry" generation. All parties with the welfare of the people at heart can co-exist in the vast panorama of India's progress. That day is coming soon.

Things may be worse before they are better. But they will be better if the people cooperate for the common good. The wholesome social, economic, political and cultural forces, released, can finally overcome the fissiparous and destructive tendencies of the land. These can build up a matchless nation for peace and progress. By the turn of the century India should be able to behold a new renaissance far exceeding all the glories of the "golden age" of Asoka and Akbar, of Greece and of Rome. With increasing know-how and unfaltering dedication the nation should be able to provide for adequate food, health, housing, education and cultural facilities for all the people. This is the greatest challenge of India's history. What a powerhouse for peace and freedom this nation can be. From the years of receiving aid India will turn to giving aid to needy nations. Morally, culturally and philanthropically the nation can engage in "ever-widening thought and action." India can, thus, help lead all mankind to a better future. It could with "tireless striving stretch its arms toward perfection" and be emblazoned in world history as a land of "truth, beauty and goodness." It could make the mightiest contribution for "peace on earth" and goodwill among nations. It would be worthy of the most idealistic traditions, worthy of its democratic foundations, worthy of the sacrifices of Tilak, Gandhi, Nehru and other leaders and, above all, worthy of the eternal spiritual power which has guided its destiny thus far.

Fervently we join with Mahatma Gandhi in his favorite prayer:

"Let us enjoy the good things of life in unity;
Let us do heroic things in unity;
Let our knowledge shine;
And let there be no hate among us."

Faithfully we look for the golden glow of a new day in India when, "Every valley shall be uplifted, and every mountain and hill shall be brought low; and the crooked shall be made straight, and the rough ways shall be made smooth."

CHAPTER XII

EPILOGUE: A BEGINNING

India has reached a crucial crossroad for her future well-being. India must immediately re-evaluate her entire politico-cultural and economic heritage. This evaluation must be performed under the criteria of consistency, desirability and practicality in terms of both domestic and foreign policy. A definitive analysis must be made of the basic principles underlying international policy, in hopes of discovering useful common denominators for a future synthesis between East and West. As for internal administration, a vital reorganization is needed, in order to utilize the vast potential lying dormant within India and to forestall a communist take-over or a military dictatorship.

Prime Minister Gandhi must face each of these problems squarely, swiftly and in a practical manner. It will require a unifying vision and a pragmatic experimental attitude. Adequate resources and knowledge are necessary.

The elections of 1967 have shaken but not shattered the progressive economic, social and political system of the Union of India. The implementation of the Fourth Plan will require several modifications, in view of changes in internal and external

210

affairs, without a change at its basis. At the same time, apart from party considerations, India must face seven major problems which will determine the country's destiny.

The first problem is that of a future harmonious development of the concept of unity in multiplicity under the impartial guardianship of the Supreme Court of India. It would be wise to examine the federal structure of the United States of America in order to note the analogous role of the U. S. Supreme Court in a historical setting and for the sake of a comparative synthesis to be applied to a concrete and detailed analysis of the past and present situation of India.

The second problem is that of finding out the upper and the lower case-limits of operation and practicality of both socialistic and free systems.

The third problem is the attitude of the communist parties to the democratic institutions and unity of India. Both communist parties (the Marxist and the Right) did not originally believe in parliamentary democracy, and the communist party of India (Marxist) caused a lot of public concern because of its submission to the ideological center of Peking, and its possible stand in a case of armed conflict between India and China. The present leadership of these parties have attempted to allay fears by affirming their primary loyalty to the people of India and disavowing subservience to any foreign country. They now have an opportunity to convince the people beyond any doubt that this is "the truth, the whole truth and nothing but the truth."

The fourth problem is that of strategic decentralization in future economic planning in terms of defensive measures, of the availability and locomotion and costs of economic resources, of present and future expansion of population, etc.

The fifth problem is that of the Community Development Program. Although its saturation has been scheduled for 1975-76, it will be wise and expedient to review the entire program in 1970 in view of past and present experiences, in order to implement its finishing phase accordingly. A desperate need in this area is a reawakening of the spirit of and confidence in Social Service.

The sixth problem is that of national language versus regional languages. This calls for great restraint and farsighted statesmanship. The language differences have grown over several millennia. These cannot be changed overnight or in one generation. Today there is so much fuss, fury and bitterness about the subject that it is untimely to press it. The concentration should be on the more urgent problems of poverty, hunger and unemployment. Under more stable conditions, a consensus should be arrived at for the solution of this most touchy problem.

The seventh and the most urgent of all problems is that of relieving the food shortage and ensuring that all precautionary measures are taken to prevent famine conditions in the future. There should be an all out mobilization of the nation for the war against hunger.

India's monumental problems require personal courage, objective firmness and strength, ideological clarity and a thorough technical preparedness in the leadership, apart from the distinct problem of having either a large or a small democratic majority in Parliament.

No doubt Indira Gandhi is facing the greatest crisis of her three-year administration. Opposition parties predict that the worst is to come. Whereas in the last election the Congress lost eight out of India's seventeen states to the opposition parties, there is the possibility according to some observers that it will lose more states in the next election unless the greatest of caution is used in handling the ministerial crises. They also predict the strong possibility of India being engulfed by communism either in a bloodless coup or a bloody revolution.

The eminent English writer Carlyle once observed that "great things turn on a straw." The cow, which is not a subject of much discussion in American politics, might become a matter of a life and death struggle in India. The whole story of cow protection is so tied up with the religion, culture and long-standing traditions of the people that anyone who handles this problem must be most careful. There is so much emotionalism attached to it that it can be real dynamite for some years in the future of India.

In the United States, Indian visitors are generally asked about the sacred cow and the rope trick. The average American is amused at all the agitation that is going on in India in the name of cow protection. In a group conversation the writer heard a young lady comment, "If I were hungry like Indians, I would chew up the first cow that I see." However, the cow problem is quite complex as we can see from a brief examination of the religious and traditional background. Implicit in Hindu religion is the notion of Karma. It means both action and the fruit (result) of action. It is through Karma that one suffers the result of evil actions, or enjoys the sweet fruits of good deeds. According to the nature of one's deeds in one life the soul reappears in other lives in the human and animal form. So, life goes on in its cycles of births and rebirths until all the results of actions are exhausted and the purified soul united with the original spiritual source from which it came. Thus, all of life is related; the same soul that resides in the human being is also in the cow. To the philosophic minded Hindu the soul can unite with the Absolute by realization, without the process of transmigration; but, for the non-philosophic and especially for the most orthodox, the traditional belief in Karma still has much relevance. Because of the belief in the transmigration of souls in animal forms and the underlying belief in the unity of all of life, destruction of animals and especially the cow has become thoroughly objectionable. The cow was the symbol of bounty, because it provided milk and milk products which nourished the body. It also provided the dung that fertilized the soil for yielding a plentiful harvest. In the early life of the Indian people, cattle formed an important part of their affluence.

Today there are nearly 72 million cows in India. Most of them are not in good condition because of the inadequacy of feed and organized care. There are nearly 27,000 cow protection shelters. A large number of old and sick cows are retired there. However, most of these shelters are inadequate in many ways to give the necessary feed and care.

One of the chief movements that tore into the Congress campaign in the last General Election and handed out a terrific beating to it is the cow protection agitation led by one of the four spiritual leaders of Hinduism, His Holiness Jagadguru Shri Shankaracharya. It was also supported by many other Holy Men of India.

Once again some Hindu leaders are threatening to agitate against the government to assure cow protection. They ask for national legislation to guarantee cows 100 percent immunity from slaughter. To date, eleven of the nation's seventeen states provide legal protection for cows. Such legislation was made possible because of pressure from the predominantly Hindu population. The government supported Council of Cow Protection has a number of projects in operation to save the cow. These are considered insufficient by the very ardent supporters of the cow population. Now they are planning a massive protest. The most influential of their leaders, Jagadguru Shankaracharya, has already threatened to "shake up the very roots of the Congress government." He probably has a larger following than any other spiritual head of India. He and his militant followers have the potential to overthrow the ministry. But the results can be disastrous. What has started in the name of cow protection could mean the destruction of the democratic foundations of India. Unwittingly the forces of compassion for the cow could play into the hands of fanatics and right-wing politicians. This will be many megatons of dynamite in their arsenal! Their ascendency to power can give ample excuse for the left-wing and especially the communists to revolt. The sum total of all this could be a civil war in which both men and cows might die by the millions.

On the other hand, the nation is moving forward on many fronts; the food problem is slowly being solved. The family planning program is progressing. The language question is being tackled with patience and deliberation. But it appears that of all problems the cow protection is the one that might get out of control! Certain factions, in spite of all their efforts, have not succeeded in overthrowing Indira Gandhi's administration; it now appears more firmly established than ever before. It has the potential to last the full five-year term and more. But, where men failed, the ''sacred'' cow might succeed. Such is the strength of emotion and sentiment tied to the cow. Two years ago, New Delhi witnessed a protest march of 200,000 under the leadership of scores of ''Holy Men'' for the protection of the ''sacred'' cow. Sporadic violence started. The revolt was put down by the firm handling of Mrs. Gandhi. The fair lady can be very firm.

The cow that eats the green grass and blesses man with white milk—the best of all foods for good health and long life—must be given loving care. If every man who talks and agitates about the cow will faithfully feed and care for just one, this land will be like Canaan of yore ''flowing with milk. . . .''

SELECTED BIBLIOGRAPHY

Agrawal, N. C., *The Food Problem of India*. Bombay: Vora and Company, 1961.

Alexander, Mithrapuram, *World Religions*. Dubuque: W. C. Brown Co., 1962.

_____, *Prince of Peace*. Dubuque: W. C. Brown Co., 1963.

_____, *Lal Bahadur Shastri*. New Delhi: New Light Publishers, 1967.

Bowles, Chester, *Ambassador's Report*. New York: Harper and Bros., 1954.

Brecher, Michael, *Nehru: A Political Biography*. London: Oxford University Press, 1962.

Chagla, M. C., *Kashmir*. Delhi: Publications Division, 1965.

Edwards, Michael, *Nehru: A Pictorial Biography*. New York: Viking Press, 1962.

Fischer, Louis, *The Life of Mahatma Gandhi*. New York: Harper and Bros., 1950.

Gandhi, M. K., *An Autobiography*. Ahmedabad: Navajivan Publishing House, 1945.

Guthrie, Anne, *Madame Ambassador*. New York: Harcourt, Brace and World Inc., 1962.

Hangan, Wells, *After Nehru, Who?* London: Rupert Hart-Davis, 1963.

Hutheesing, Krishna (Nehru), *With No Regrets*. New York: John Day, 1945.

—————————————, *We Nehrus*. New York: Holt, 1967.

Information Service of India, *India*. Washington: Embassy of India, 1965.

—————————————, *India News*. Vols. II, III, IV, V. Washington: Embassy of India, 1963-1966.

Mankekar, D. R., *Lal Bahadur*. Bombay: Popular Prakashan, 1964.

—————————————, *Twenty-Two Fateful Days*. Bombay: P. C. Manaktola and Sons, 1966.

Maxmuller, F., *Sacred Books of the East Series*. Vols. I and XV, *The Upanishads,* Oxford: Oxford University Press, 1879-1900.

Menon, V. P., *Transfer of Power in India*. Princeton: Princeton University Press, 1957.

Moraes, Frank, *India Today*. New York: Macmillan Company, 1960.

Moreland, W. H. and Chatterjee, A. C., *A Short History of India*. New York: Longmans and Green, 1953.

Muzumdar, Haridas T., *Mahatma Gandhi*. Ahmedabad: Navajivan Publishing House, 1962.

Nanda, B. R., *Mahatma Gandhi: A Biography*. Boston: Beacon Press, 1958.

—————————————, *The Nehrus, Motilal and Jawaharlal*. London: Allen and Unwin, 1963.

Nehru, Jawaharlal, *The Discovery of India*. New York: John Day, 1942.

—————————————, *A Bunch of Old Letters*. Bombay: Asia Publishing House, 1958.

—————————————, *Nehru on World History*. New York: John Day, 1960.

——————————————, *Toward Freedom*. New York: John Day, 1941.

——————————————, *Nehru, The First Sixty Years*. New York: John Day, 1965.

——————————————, *Independence and After*. New York: John Day, 1941.

——————————————, *The Unity of India*. New York: John Day, 1942.

Panikkar, K. M., *Common Sense About India*. London: Victor Gollancz, 1960.

Publications Division, *India—A Reference Manual*. New Delhi: Ministry of Information and Broadcasting, 1965.

——————————————, *Speeches*. Delhi: Lal Bahadur Shastri, 1965.

——————————————, *The Chinese Aggression: Combo Proposals*. Delhi: Ministry of Information and Broadcasting, September, 1965.

——————————————, *Mahatma Gandhi and One World*. New Delhi: Ministry of Information and Broadcasting, 1966.

——————————————, *The Collected Works of Mahatma Gandhi* (14 Volumes). Delhi: Ministry of Information and Broadcasting, 1945.

Radhaskrishnan, S., *Hindu View of Life*. London: Allen and Unwin, 1927.

Sahgal, Nayantara, *Prison and Chocolate Cake*. New York: Alfred A. Knopf, 1954.

Schweitzer, Albert, *Indian Thought and Its Development*. Lord, Hodder, and Stoughton, 1936.

Singh, Anup, *The Rising Star of India*. London: Allen and Unwin, 1940.

Sheean, Vincent, *Nehru: The Years of Power*. New York: Random House, 1960.

Shridharani, K. J., *My India, My America. New* York: Duelle, Sloane and Pierce, 1941.

Smith, Donald, *India as a Secular State*. Princeton: Princeton University Press, 1963.

Souvenir Volumes Committee, *Jawaharlal Nehru: A Memorial Album*. Bombay: Popular Prakashan, 1965.

Tendulkar, D. G., *Mahatma* (8 volumes). Bombay: Thacri and Tendulkar, 1954.

Tennyson, Hallem, *India's Walking Saint*. New York: Doubleday Company, 1955.

Wallbank, Thomas Walter, *India, A Survey of the Heritage and Growth of Indian Nationalism*. New York: Holt, 1948.

GLOSSARY OF INDIAN WORDS

Arjun—Disciple of Lord Krishna and leading member of the Pandava family in the Epic, *Mahabharata.*

Ashram—A retreat.

Balsahayog—A training center for destitute children in Delhi.

Bhagavad Gita—Literally, Song of the Lord. It is an abstract of the philosophical teachings of Hinduism pertaining especially to duty.

Brahmin— a member of the priestly class.

Crore—Ten million.

Dadu—Grandfather.

Dalai Lama—Spiritual head of Buddhists, who headed the State of Tibet before the occupation of the Chinese.

Ji—Affixed to the names of persons as a sign of respect.

Kurukshetra—Battlefield in which Pandava and Kaurava families fought (as narrated in the Epic, *Mahabharata*).

Lathi—Long stick tipped with lead.

Mahamela—Literally "great festival"; the day on which thousands of people gather for immersion in the Ganges.

Maharani—Queen.

Mahatma—Great Soul.

Marthoma—St. Thomas.

Munshi—A clerk, and in some cases, a language teacher.

Pakora—Fritter.

Panch Sheel—Five principles of peaceful coexistence.

Pandit—Scholar, also a title given to the Nehru family.

Panchayat—Village council.

Papu—Father.

Pathan—Member of a warrior tribe located in Afghanistan.

Quid-I-Azam—Saviour of the People.

Ramayan—One of the two great epics of India.

Rupee—Monetary unit in India (7½ Rs. = $1.00).

Sari—The garment worn by Indian women.

Satyagraha—Truth force. The name used by Mahatma Gandhi for non-violent non-cooperation during the freedom struggle.

Swaraj—Self-government.

Veda—Ancient scriptures of the Hindus.

Yoga—A system of mental and physical discipline.

INDEX